To
GOD
Be the
GLORY

Bruce E. Wright

ISBN 978-1-0980-1551-0 (paperback)
ISBN 978-1-0980-1552-7 (digital)

Christian Faith Publishing, Inc.
832 Park Avenue
Meadville, PA 16335
www.christianfaithpublishing.com

Printed in the United States of America

ACKNOWLEDGMENTS

To my beautiful and loving wife, Sandy, who gave me the inspiration and encouragement to write.

To Pastor Dave Burton who did some typing for me and rearranged some sentences to make them flow better.

Excerpts from books from Max Lucado and Dee Henderson.

A reader's forum article by Eric Jefferies.

To my wonderful sister-in-law Connie Wright who did a lot of typing for me and gave me some good ideas.

Most of all, I thank our *great* God who kept reminding me of things to write. May this give him honor and glory.

Luke 1-37

For with God, nothing shall be impossible.

Bruce E. Wright

Notes to Bruce from Pastor Burton

You have written a great story! Writing from "inside your feelings" has made this a great story. Merely writing facts such as, "I went to grade school and my teacher was…" is not what this story is about. Wonderful! Telling stories of your hurts and of your reactions make upgrades on this essay. In fact, some paragraphs were wonderfully emotional. The writing has the author inside the character.

PREFACE

How could I find a better way to start giving God glory than with the old hymn of the church "To God Be the Glory"?

> To God be the glory great things He hath done! So loved He the world that He gave us His Son, who yielded His life an atonement for sin and opened the Life gate that all may go in.
>
> Praise the Lord, Praise the Lord, Let the earth hear His voice! Praise the Lord, Praise the Lord, Let the people rejoice! Come to the Father through Jesus the Son and give Him the glory great things. He hath done!
>
> O perfect redemption, the purchase of blood! To every believer the promise of God; The vilest offender who truly believes, that moment from Jesus a pardon receives.
>
> Praise the Lord, Praise the Lord, Let the earth hear His voice! Praise the Lord, Praise the Lord, Let the people rejoice! Come to the Father thru Jesus the Son, and give him the glory great things He hath done!
>
> Great things He hath taught us, great things He hath done, and great our rejoicing thru Jesus the Son, but purer and higher and greater will be our wonder, our transport, when Jesus we see.
>
> Praise the Lord, Praise the Lord, Let the earth hear His voice! Praise the Lord, Praise the Lord, let the people rejoice! Come to the Father

thru Jesus the Son, and give Him the glory great
thing He hath done!

Isn't that a great hymn? Underneath the title in the song book, it says it comes from Psalms 126. I would have said it came from Psalms 66, but that's just my own opinion.

BE THE GLORY

Some people think we need to justify God, but they are wrong. God is God, and the Creator doesn't need to be justified. God just wants us to tell people all that He has done for us. Everything that happens to us can be part of our testimony. God has done so much for me, I had better write segments of my life so I can say thank you to him for all he's done for me.

I am Bruce Wright, and I am seventy-three years old. I am writing these segments of my life not to show what great things I have done. The truth of the matter is, I have done no outstanding things in these seventy-three years. I am writing this so you can see how God works His *loving* miracles throughout the lives of those who love and serve Him.

Jesus, the author of our life, is also the finisher of our life story. He was there when we were born, and He is there each step of the way. He is here in my life, chapter by chapter, 'til I draw my final breath and my life story comes to an end. When we stand with Christ in *glory* looking over life's finished story, then, Lord, shall I fully know how much I owe. Will my life tell the story of Christ's love and mercy to the world around me?

I was born April 2, 1938, to George C. Wright and Vida K. (Greensides) Wright. I was the sixth child of seven. Naomi was the oldest; I was all the time kidding her by reminding her that her name was on the toilet, which it was, because the trade name printed on the toilet was Naomi.

Duane was the next oldest. He could be gruff, but he had a tender heart. One time my mother's washing machine quit working, Duane quit also—quit school, that is. He quit school and got a job so he could buy my mother a new washing machine. She could not talk him into going back to school until he had bought her that washing machine.

Marguerite was the next oldest. We called her Peggy because that was much easier to pronounce and spell. If I got mad at her, being the little brat I was, I would call her Piggy.

June was number four among us kids. When June was perhaps six years old, she developed pneumonia and measles, which affected her brain so that her brain did not mature beyond the age of ten. However, she made some of the most beautiful rugs you would ever see. She had the knack of making both sides the same so you couldn't tell the top from the bottom.

Joan was the next child. She and I were very close; she probably was my favorite. After Mom died, we became even closer. One year after she received her income tax money, she bought my first bicycle I ever had. That was pretty nice for a sixteen-year-old sister.

Dennis was the youngest in the family. He was only nine months old when our mother died. My sister Peggy and her husband Roland raised Dennis. We also had a half-brother, David, the son of my father from his first marriage. David never seemed like "half" of anything. He and his wife, Ruby, made one sweet couple. He was as much of a brother as the other two.

The first time I remember seeing them I was about five years old. They came to visit us. There was David, Ruby, their son, David, and their adopted daughter, Pam. I don't remember much about that visit. I remember sitting around the living room talking, but that is it. Ruby said the first time she saw me, I came in the house, and my face was pure black. All she could see was the whites of my eyes and my white teeth. She asked me where I'd been, and I said I had been helping a friend shovel coal. I have to take her word for it, I don't remember. I wish I could remember more about my early life, but the few things I remember are the bits and pieces the Lord helps me remember. After Mom died, it was so painful that I pushed all my hurts to the far back reaches of my mind where the pain couldn't hurt me anymore. The thing I regret most is the good times went with the bad.

The Lord has been wonderful to help me remember some things from the past as I am writing this, both the good times and the hurtful.

I am looking forward to the time when we go home and there will be no past, just the present and all the love-filled time spent with Jesus.

Leaving the future and getting back to the past. The next time I remember David and his family was at Mom's funeral. We were going to the cemetery. I made the comment, "Mom died of a blood clot on the brain. That's the same thing President Roosevelt died of."

David sobbed and said, "They were both great people."

David and his family moved around quite a bit. They lived at Flagstaff, Arizona, for a while. They were in Kalamazoo, Michigan, for a while. David was a cook at the University of Kalamazoo. Dad and I went to see them, and David gave us a tour of his kitchen. It was quite impressive.

Their final place to call home was in Texas. It is a small place outside of Houston, Texas. Sandy and I called them and told them we were going to be on vacation and would like to come and see them and maybe go into Mexico. They said they would love to see us come, and we never did see Mexico.

It was a long trip, but Sandy and I didn't get tired driving. I don't think we drove once. Paul had just gotten his driving permit, so he and Bruce took turns driving. David and Ruby were glad to see us, and we had a great time. One day we went to the Johnson Space Center. There was sure a lot to see. Another day we went to Galveston and had a picnic. The boys and their uncle David fished. Two nights we went into Houston and watched ballgames. We had such a good time with them. It was surprising that although they were in their sixties we had all we could do to keep up with them.

The boys, David, and I would stayed up half the night playing cribbage; it seemed like we didn't get tired of it. As we were playing, I sometimes got lost in the fact that he looked so much like how Dad had looked. It was almost like playing cards with Dad. I am not sure, but I might have slipped and called him dad once or twice.

It seemed like we just got there, and I had such a good time with them, but now it was time to get on the road and go home. It's the only time I can remember being on vacation and not be glad I was heading home to my own bed.

It was not a long time later that David died of a brain tumor. Ruby made the comment a short time after, that now that David was gone, we would probably forget her. We told her we would never forget her. We try to call her once in a while and talk to her. She is such a sweetheart.

Their adopted daughter, Pam, is dead now. She has been dead for quite a while, but Pam's daughter Shawna is still alive. David and Ruby have a daughter, Janine. She is still alive and visits her mother when she gets a chance.

They have one son, David, who's alive and working for God. A friend of his got the idea to start a biker's church. He started one even though his heart really wasn't in it, and David helped him by preaching sometimes and helping with the administration part of the church.

One day David was supposed to preach. The friend said, "Before you start preaching, could I get up and say a few words?"

David said, "Sure it's your church. Do what you like." The friend got up and told the congregation that his heart really wasn't into running a church, so now it was David's church. He walked out, and it became David running God's church for the Father.

I asked David if he ever sees his friend. He told me he sees him every so often, and they are still friends.

David's wife told him, "David, you are now doing what I told you a long time ago. You were meant to be a minister for God."

It's been quite a few years that have gone by, and he is still a faithful servant of God. The biker's church that started with eight members every Sunday now averages about one hundred members. David told me if everyone came every Sunday, they would average between 180 and 200 members. The reason there is such a big difference is that some of them work on the oil rigs and work some Sundays. There are also some who aren't Christians yet and some that haven't matured in the Lord yet, and the world may still be distracting them some Sundays.

You might think that because it is a biker's church, that it is all adults. That is far from the truth. They have kids of all ages. It is like most churches, they have those kids that come with their parents, those their parents send, and those they go and get.

They have programs for young kids, and they also have a youth group. The program for the kids is three years old and up.

They also send kids thirteen-year-olds and older to camp. The kids don't have to pay to go to camp because the church pays their way. David told me they had just had a fish fry that they made $1,000 on. That money would be used toward sending kids to camp. The cost for the camp is $250 a child, so they earned enough to send four children to camp with just one event. They also have a biker's group called "The Sons of Thunder." It takes its name from the fact Jesus called James and John "the sons of thunder." He told me they go out riding every so often and witness to people. He says the evangelistic part of ministry is what he enjoys the most.

David shared with me the stories of a couple of people I would consider a real challenge, but when you put your faith in Jesus, it makes all the difference in the world. For with God, nothing shall be impossible (Luke 1:37).

He told me one lesbian and her adopted son came to the church. She told David after a while that she wanted to become a Christian. David told her she would have to end the relationships she was in. She asked David what would happen to her son if something happened to her. He said, "I will take your son." She ended her relationships and gave her heart to Jesus. Her son now calls David "Pastor Dad." What a heartwarming story.

Another time, a Jehovah's Witness came to his door, he told David he was a Jehovah's Witness and asked David if he could talk to him. David told him he was a pastor and we are all called to be witnesses for our great God Jehovah, but the only way to get to him is by the way of his son Jesus. The Jehovah's Witness saw he was not going to get anywhere with this pastor, so he left. He was kind of curious, so one Sunday, he came to church, and he found Jesus and was saved.

I only talked to David a short time so he could not tell me all there was to tell, and I probably forgot some of what he did tell me, but you can see what happens when you trust in God and do his work.

Ten years have come and gone, and I know David couldn't tell me everything there is to tell in the short time we talked. One thing is for sure, he doesn't regret one moment of all these years of faithful service to the Lord. When you are called by God to serve him and never look back, it is an honor to serve our great God. I am sure David would add a loud *amen*.

Now we come to my parents. What I can tell you about them is very little and mostly what other people have told me. My dad had several lines of work. Over the years, he drove bus, drove taxi, and was a shoemaker. He was not much of a father or a husband. He gave my mother only $5 toward caring for the family. In the evening, he liked to go over to the neighborhood bar and play cards. When he came home from the bar or on an evening when he didn't go to the bar, he would lay on the couch and fall asleep—if he could. My sisters loved to roll his hair in clothespins. He didn't have an angry bone in his body. He just let them have their fun. It may have been because they were his "little girls."

Sometimes my dad took me fishing, but most often, I went fishing alone. I probably shouldn't have gone without someone with me. "Why?" you ask me. "Because I was seven or eight years old and was too young to fear the dangers the water holds for someone who can't swim." One day I fell into the water and would have drowned except a man who was working nearby realized he had not seen me for a minute or two and came, found me struggling, and lifted me out of the water.

Another time I learned to fear and respect the water was one evening when my brother Duane my dog Tip, and I were walking on the ice. We had walked quite a distance from shore when our dog, Tip, fell through a hole in the ice. Duane tried to rescue him and fell into the water himself. After struggling for a while, Duane climbed onto the ice and also rescued Tip. They were wet and cold and ran for home. As I followed them, I was afraid I would fall into a hole in the ice because it was getting dark, but Duane yelled to me and said, "Just keep coming in this direction." I was so afraid that I walked as though walking on eggs. I was never so happy in all my life as when I got near to the shore and saw my sister Peggy waiting for me.

I have another lasting memory of my dad. One day after my mom died, my dad said, "If you get the dishes done after school, I will take you to the movies." When school was over, some of the guys wanted me to play football with them. I felt I had plenty of time to play for a while and still get the dishes done before Dad arrived. Before I knew it, it was five o'clock, and Dad was already home. He went to the movies without me. He taught me a good lesson, right? When I arrived in school the next day, one of my classmates told me my dad had taken him to the movies. The only lesson I learned was that I wasn't any more important to him than one of the neighborhood boys. I don't hate my dad—I really didn't know him.

I didn't know anything about Dad's childhood and nor did I know anything about his growing up years. In fact, I didn't know much about his adult years either. What I do know is that he was not much of a husband. My mother and dad were an unlikely pair. Dad was sixteen years older than Mom and with only a sixth grade education, while my mother had a college degree. They say that "love is blind." I guess this match proves the saying to be true.

My mom was a super person, the mother of seven children. She worked full time outside the home from nine o'clock to six o'clock. To earn extra money, at night, she took in ironing. After all of this, she had time for us kids who loved her very much—except Naomi. After we were adults and I had married Sandy, we visited Naomi and her family. She frequently bad-mouthed our mother to Sandy. One day Sandy said to Naomi, "If you want to have a good relationship with your brother, you better not say anything bad about your mother to him."

Naomi was always kind of wild when she was young. Also she made very poor decisions at times. For instance, once she ran the phone bill to over $100, and my mother let her have it! Naomi didn't understand that a woman with seven kids, struggling to make ends meet, wasn't going to give her hugs and kisses for laying a $100 bill on top of everything else.

Another time when I was six or seven, Naomi took me across Lake Michigan on the car ferry without telling anyone, not even my mother. I don't know if she called home from Wisconsin or not, but my mother was upset and angry with her. Naomi didn't use very good judgment when she was younger. She just couldn't understand why mother got so upset with her. I think as Naomi grew older, she became wiser. She married and became a Christian. I am not sure if that was the order. But isn't it nice that God can work miracle in people's lives? It is no wonder that Dad was Naomi's favorite parent—he never disciplined us kids.

Like everything else, disciplining was Mom's job. Mom believed in the old fashion adage: "Spare the rod and spoil the child." When one of us did something wrong, we felt the "ruler of correction." When one of us did something wrong and would not admit it, we all lined up and were punished. This may seem like harsh punishment, but what would you do if you were a mother of seven kids and had no help from your husband? Maybe my mother's loving discipline kept me from not winding up in a prison as I grew older.

As if it weren't bad enough, my mother had to deal with June also. June started running away. She also began taking things that didn't belong to her and began lying. The straw that broke the camel's back was when she went into the house of a single man; that was a place she should not have been. It seemed that caring for June was a full-time job. My mother felt she had no choice but to put June into a home for mentally challenged at the age of eleven. It seemed as though with June gone, the bad things that happened slowed down and so did the punishments. I don't think June understood why she was put into the home, and I don't think she ever understood why she could never return home. I think that as long as June lives, she will always want to come back home, never realizing home—as she knew it—no longer exists. Someday she will be able to go home and be with her *heavenly* Father. It will be a far better home there than the one she was cheated out of so many years ago.

I talked with Peggy's daughter Karen the other day. She told me that her mother told her I gave her the nickname of Peggy. That's kind of ironic; Peggy gave me a Bugs Bunny bank for Christmas when I was little. I grew to love Bugs and would go around the house saying, "What's up, Doc?" Someone gave me the nickname of Doc. My sisters Naomi and Joan called me Doc until the day they die. My sister who was responsible for my getting the nickname of Doc called me Brucie all her life.

My mother would send us kids to Sunday school every Sunday except for the Sundays my dad took me fishing with him. That would make my mother very upset with him. I think she knew we needed more Sunday school and less fishing. In all fairness to my dad, I think I pestered him until he finally said, "Yes, you can go."

My mom and dad went to church the usual times most non-Christians go: Christmas and Easter. My dad told me when I was grown that he and my mother both believed in reincarnation. I wish I had been a Christian back then so I could have told them the Bible tells us "and it is appointed onto men once to die and after that the judgment." I could have told them, but it was a long time after this that I became a Christian and learned the Bible truths for myself.

In 1949, when I was eleven years old, I saved S & H Green stamps. In November or December, I finally got a book full. I got a double boiler for my mom for Christmas with that book of stamps. My mother had severe headaches for several weeks in November and December of 1949. She couldn't seem to get rid of them, but that didn't stop her from going to work every day. She came home the night of the twenty-third of December with her head aching so bad that she could hardly think. As the night went on, her headache got worse. I said, "Mom, why don't you open the present I got you?"

"No," Mom said. "We'll wait 'til Christmas."

My dad called the doctor, and he sent an ambulance to take Mom to the hospital. They laid her onto the gurney and carried her out of the house. I looked out the window and watched them load her into the ambulance. As I watched it drive through the snow, I knew I would never see her alive again. The next day, I was told Mom died just before midnight. Mom was gone and so was Christmas.

Like everything else, Christmas was left to my mother. She evidently had such severe headaches that she put off buying presents. Mom was like the glue that held our family together. So without Mom, the family fell apart. My sister Naomi had married and lived in Coon Rapids, Minnesota, with her husband, Wally. Later they had a son, Bruce; a daughter, Cindy; and an adopted daughter, Carol. Naomi asked me to come out and live with them. I thanked her and told her no. All my friends were here in Michigan.

Peggy was already married to Roland J. Anthony. Dad asked them if they would take Denny who was nine months old. They accepted him and raised Denny as their very own. They would have adopted him, but Duane caused a fuss. He felt Denny should keep the Wright name.

At the age of nineteen, Duane married his girlfriend, Pat Blucker, who was eighteen. They moved into our house to try to hold the remnant of the family together. But Joan, fifteen, and I, at the age of eleven, wouldn't let Pat rule over us when she was not that much older than we. In our mind, she was not going to take our mother's place. Dad paid the bills, and Pat ruled the roost with Duane backing her. After a short time of family turmoil, Dad and Duane mutually agreed that he and Pat would leave our home.

Joan began looking out for us in the best way she could. She went to school, worked part-time, made meals, did the washing, and tried to look out for her brother who had a mind of his own. This wasn't the normal family, but things seemed to run smoother.

All my friends had to be at home at nine o'clock each evening. I stayed out longer; why should I go home when there was no one there? A lonely house is no fun to go home to. Because I could stay out later than my friends, they envied me. After my friends went inside their homes, I would roam the neighborhood. I could see through their windows and see them interacting with each other. They didn't know it, but I envied them more than they envied me.

I didn't go to Sunday school anymore though I still believed in God. I would lay on my bed in the winter and talk to God. In the summers, I would lay out in the grass and look up at the stars and talk to Him. I'd ask Him Why He took my mom to heaven. He knew how much I missed and needed her. He never answered me, but I always felt better afterward. I didn't know for sure back then if God really heard me or not. But as I look back, I can see He was already at work on my behalf.

God sent a retired man from Dow and his wife into our neighborhood, Mr. and Mrs. Perry—such a nice couple. He made bases for our baseball field. He also made a backstop that was mostly to protect his workshop windows more than to stop our balls. Although he was nice, he had one glaring fault—he saw me as the nasty little brat that I was. His wife though was a very special lady who looked beyond all my faults. She saw an eleven-year-old boy who needed some loving. She took me to bingo on Wednesday nights. She washed behind my ears and gave me a dollar so I could go to the Shrine Circus with the rest of my class. She also made little jobs around her house for me to do. Her husband could have done those jobs, but she wanted to let me do them so she could give me a little spending money.

One time I arrived at her house a little late (probably because I had been playing ball). Her husband started grumbling, and she just said to him, "Now, Clarence!" Although my brother's wife Pat was too young to take the place of my mother, this lady, Mrs. Perry, could stand in for Mom. She didn't try to boss me around; she just showed me the kind of love and friendship only a mother can give.

As I write this, I just talked to God. I told him I didn't know if Mrs. Perry was a Christian, but I hoped He had her in heaven with Him, because she showed me the kind of love He demands of us Christians.

CHAPTER 1

When I was in eighth grade, three of us boys, Billy Lange, Harry Fargo, and I went out for a boat ride. Billy was operating the motor, Harry sat in the middle of the boat, and I sat up front. When we came back to the dock, Billy didn't shut the motor off in time. I put my hand on the dock to stop the boat, but it didn't stop. My hand smashed between the boat and the dock. The impact laid the flesh open on my thumb. My hand was hit so hard with such force, it popped a whole open on the back of my hand. All three of us were in shock. We just sat there! Finally a man on the bridge yelled to us, saying, "You kids better get him to the hospital!" We climbed out of the boat and started running toward fourth ward where the hospital was located. After a couple of blocks, I could not run any further, so we slowed down to a walk. When we got to the hospital, someone called our family doctor. He came and sewed up my thumb with twenty-three stitches to seal the wound. That was the first time I ever stayed overnight at the hospital.

I had two other injuries during my childhood. The first accident was with a glass in a door. The glass had been broken and never fixed. I don't remember why, but I stuck my arm through the hole in the glass and sliced my arm. I remember it bled heavy, and the cells were coming out. I don't remember if we could not afford the hospital or if the doctors just did not do much stitching. I still have a two-inch scar on my arm.

The third injury I remember was when I knelt on the broken rim of a fruit jar. I couldn't have been more than six or seven years old. I was the only one home, and I was sure I was going to die. It wasn't long after I had this thought that my sister came home from work. She assured me I was not going to die. I felt much better.

I just remembered one more thing that happened when I was seven or eight. I got a cap gun for Christmas. It was the nicest cap gun I ever had. It had a cylinder that could spin around like a real gun. You could open the gun up and put a disc of caps in, then close it up.

The cylinder would turn when you pulled the trigger, and you could shoot six times before reloading. Just like a real gun.

One day in the spring, I was down by the lake. I had my trusty six-shooter with me. Two older boys took it away from me. They wouldn't give it back; they just kept teasing me. One of them found an old pillow and some string. They tied the string to the pillow, laid the gun on the pillow, and floated it out into the water. After a while, they got tired of teasing me, or maybe listening to me cry. They brought the gun back in and gave it back to me. My trusty six-shooter was never the same again. It had gotten wet, and after some time, it started rusting. I don't remember any more about my pistol, but I was thinking the other day about a program I watch on TV called *American Restoration*. People bring in things that are nothing but junk, and when they get done with it, it is as good as new. It is unbelievable. I also thought that even as eye-popping as that is, I thought of something that is even more amazing. Jesus takes our broken and busted lives and turns them into a thing of beauty, and unlike all those things that are restored, when this old world is gone, we will not die; we will live forever. How's that for restoration.

As I am writing this, a movie is playing on TV starring Kevin Costner called *For the Love of the Game*. I've always had a love for baseball as long as I can remember. My friend Gary and I always played against Ron and Roger Fredericks. One day we got into an argument about something. Roger had his bat resting on his shoulder. I tugged on it, not a hard tug, but Roger had an excuse to get his mom involved. He went crying into the house. His mother came out getting all over me for picking on her little darlings. When she finally got done long enough to get her second wind, Gary and I started walking toward his house. She was still tattling on as we walked out of hearing range. Suddenly I heard Gary's dad call my name. I was sure I was going to hear it all over again. When I turn and looked at him, he just smiled and said, "You aren't hurting those wild Indians, are you?" If I never loved that man before, I sure did after that. I think the love of the game was at its highest peak when I formed a softball team so I could play softball with my two sons.

I am sure it was God who sent Mr. and Mrs. Perry into my life to keep me from getting into too much trouble after Mom died. But in my later teen years, Mrs. Perry's love just wasn't enough. I cried out to God to send me someone to love so I could have a home too. I found out one thing about God: He doesn't do things halfway. He sent a young Christian girl into my life named Sandy. She became my wife and best friend. She gave me two sons who married two fine ladies. They gave me five wonderful grandchildren. I always say, "How is that for turning lemons into lemonade?"

Sandy was four and a half years younger than me, but to tell you the truth, she was more mature than I was. We went together for seven years. Part of the reason we dated so long was that she was still in school. When she got out of school, I was drafted into the service. It was hard being away from home for two years. Being away from my future wife and best friend was even harder.

I was twenty-three years old when I was drafted. I went to Detroit for my physical, returned home for a few days, and then went to Fort Knox, Kentucky, for my basic training.

I was there for six weeks and returned home for a short time. I then went to Fort Chaffey, Arkansas. It was right outside of Fort Smith. We were there another six weeks getting our advance infantry training. We then headed for Baumholder, Germany. I weighed 130 pounds soaking wet when I entered the service. I was 155 pounds when I came out. I was in Germany only nine days when my dad died of prostate cancer. I came back home for thirty days before returning to Germany. This was about the same time of the Berlin crisis; we did a lot of training while we were in Germany. After eight months, we rotated back to the States. It was cold when we left Germany to arrive in Fort Benning, Georgia, in the afternoon with the temperature at eighty. We weren't in Georgia very long before we went on a twenty-four-hour alert. It was when they had the "Bay of Pigs" invasion. Not very long after that, we had to pack up and go to Fort McClellan, Alabama, where they had the Birmingham riots. That was the most exciting activity we had outside of playing war games. My only combat injury happened just twenty-seven days before I got out of the service. Four or five of us guys were putting school desks together when I slipped on a piece of cardboard and jammed my finger into the hole the top set in. The tendon in my finger was torn. It was never repaired, and I can't bend that finger, but it has not hurt me over the years.

If I were to name the two people from my army days who had the biggest impact on me, I would have to say Joe Gerngross and Sergeant Noah. Joe was my best friend; Joe had only been in the States for a year when he was drafted. We became close friends. In fact, years later, Joe told Sandy we were so close he almost married me. He was joking of course.

One time when we were in Germany, we went down to Baumholder. We didn't do a whole lot; we just got a bite to eat and looked around. When we got back to the base, we had to turn our passes in to the officer of the day, who was a friend of ours. I pretended I was drunk. I staggered around and slurred my speech. The officer of the day said, "Oh no, not you too Wright?" We started laughing, and he knew he had been had.

Another time we were on war games. We were aggressing against the eighteenth infantry. It was getting dark as we set up camp. We had three men teams around the perimeter. Sergeant Archie, Joe, and I were one team. Joe and Sergeant Archie went back to our personal carrier and got their sleeping bags. When they returned, I went and got mine. I leaned my rifle against a tree when I left, and when I returned, I couldn't find it. My night vision is very poor. I stumbled around looking for my rifle and stepped off into a mud hole. I went in up to my waist. I was wet and miserable for two days. I finally climbed up on our vehicle while the motor was running. I straddled the manifold until the mud dried and then tapped it off my pants. What a difference that made. I could get in my sleeping bag to sleep at night. That manifold served different purposes. When we were in the field, our food was C rations. They weren't too bad, but some of them were pretty greasy when they were cold. For instance, lima beans and ham had a half inch of grease on top. We would open the cans and set them by the manifold and heat them, and then they were pretty good.

Another time I remember, we were warring against the 101 airborne. It was getting late as we were setting up camp. We had the same three-man teams. I was with Sergeant Archie and Joe. By the time we all got in position and set up, it was dark. It had only been about a half hour when we heard a crack, like someone had stepped on a twig. Joe said, "Oh, oh, they're coming." Joe had a few blanks left from our last encounter. I was out of ammo.

As they got close enough so that we could see them, Joe shot the rest of his blanks, and I stuck out my finger and started yelling, "Bang, bang, bang." The airborne had an umpire with them. I always wondered how many kills Joe got for his blanks or how many I got for my smoking finger. Joe and I always got a laugh over it anyway.

One Sunday morning after we had exercised and we finished breakfast, we were told to pack our gear; we were going on a mission behind enemy lines. We were loaded into helicopters and headed out for our drop behind the 101 airborne's lines. It was about a half-hour ride, and we landed behind their lines. It was a surprise, but the surprise was not theirs; it was ours. When we landed, two tanks had our helicopter surrounded. We jumped out of the helicopter and headed into the woods. We ran around the woods for about an hour and a half. They finally ran us out into a clearing where their troops were eating. Trays went flying, and they grabbed their guns. They had us captured. They questioned us for about a half hour and then took us to our Bravo Company's lines and released us.

Lieutenant Simms was our platoon leader. He was a second lieutenant right out of ROTC. He couldn't read a map very well, and he was always in trouble with the company commander. This time however, he was the company commander. All the other officers of the company were still captured. Commander Simms made a decision that endeared him to us. We hadn't eaten since breakfast, and so we were starved. He took us to the nearest guesthouse. A guesthouse was a cross between a hotel and a restaurant. There were shrubs all the way around it, and the road out front was a runway for the airborne. We lay behind the shrubs and ate sandwiches waiting for our vehicles to come and pick us up. When they finally came, some of us were sleeping. They woke us up, and we went to our vehicles that were parked behind the guesthouse. We took a roll call, and everyone was there except for Lancaster. Someone went back to wake Lancaster, but he was not there. We found out the next day what happened to Lancaster. He woke up, and thinking we were out front, he ran out and was captured for the second time that day. I think that must be some kind of record.

I remember one time when we were going on maneuvers, our personal carrier quit. Sergeant Garcia's vehicle pulled up, and the Sarge told Sergeant Bradley we could get into theirs and ride with them. They had the hatch open, and Sergeant Garcia was standing up and watching out the hatch. Sergeant Bradley joined him top side. Sergeant Bradley was always chewing tobacco. He kept spitting, and the wind was blowing it in Sergeant Garcia's face. He kept wiping his face, and he was getting madder and madder. He finally told Sergeant Bradley, "If you spit one more time, you are getting out and walk." Sergeant Bradley wasn't very smart. I think he was in the army because he couldn't: make it in the outside world, but he was smart enough not to spit anymore.

The last memory I had of Germany was the last outing we were on. They told us we were going on a river crossing. That was an experience. We battened down the hatch and started across the river. The carrier was shaking like crazy. I thought sure it was going to fall apart. Water started dripping off the hatch, and I was sure we were going to drown. I was never so glad in all my life as when we made land on the other side. I am sure I felt like kissing the ground, but I didn't.

One day we got the news that our outfit was rotating back to the states. That sure was good news. We had been in Germany for eight months. We would be going to Fort Benning, Georgia. When we left Germany in the morning, it was forty-five degrees, and when we reach Fort Benning in the afternoon, it was eighty degrees. What a change that was.

Most of us were no longer in the infantry. We were in headquarters company. I was in the three-man team again. This time, I was on a gun jeep; I was the gunner. Our first action was in a maneuver called Swiss Strike. We didn't see much action. Our job was guarding the colonel and his jeep. Where the colonel went, we went. It was a dirty job. It really was a dirty job.

Every day the colonel had to go back to brigade headquarters to meet with the other officers and plan strategy. His jeep would lead and ours followed. It was a dirt road, and we ate his dust both ways coming and going. I can almost still feel the dirt gritting in my teeth. One night, the things changed. We were going to have to run a roadblock. This time, they put our jeep first. We could see a four-way stop ahead, so we gunned the engine raced through. As we entered the intersection, a machine gun started firing. I could feel the effects of the blanks tapping on my leg. I know that if those bullets would have been real, they would have cut my leg in two. I thank God I never had to be in any real combat. They say that war is hell. When I see the condition of a lot of our boys that come home and a lot that never make it home, it's pretty close.

My buddy Joe and I have kept in contact over the years. Joe's wife was from the Ukraine. People would say to her, "How could you marry him after what the Germans did to your country. You even lost your dad." She would tell them, "Joe had nothing to do with it. He was just a little boy."

Joe and his wife have two children, a boy and a girl. The last few years, Joe has gone through a lot. He lost his wife, his sister, and his son-in-law. He had heart surgery and a stroke. When I talk to him, he has a hard time grasping for words. Some of the words that come out of his mouth aren't pretty. They don't glorify God. I pray that he will find the Lord. I know he goes to church, but I love Joe, and I just would like him to find a close relationship with the Lord and allow the Lord to change him. Romans 12 says, "And be not conformed to this world, but be transformed by the renewing of your mind. Then you will be able to know what is the good and pleasing perfect will of God." I pray for Joe every day. I want to be with him in heaven someday.

Sergeant Noah taught me about myself. We were going on a field trip that ended on top of a mile-high hill. I always did what was easy. I wasn't going to college, so in high school, I took all the easy courses. I would begin doing things, but if they started to become difficult, I'd quit. We started up this hill, and I began working up a sweat. There is a code between quitters: "Never be the first to drop out." I looked around and saw guys dropping out, so I started heading for the side of the road. Sergeant Noah came up beside me and said, "Come on, Wright, you can make it."

"No, I can't," I said. "The sky is purple, and the sun went behind the moon."

Quitters look for whatever they think of as a reason to give up. Sergeant Noah wouldn't let me give up. He just kept talking to me, and before I knew it, we were on the top of the hill. I was sweaty, I was tired, but I made it to the top of the hill. I looked down the hill to those quitters and smiled. I knew I was never going to be one of them again. Sergeant Noah helped change my life forever, but he will never know unless I meet him in heaven. There is one more person from my army days that holds a spot in my heart. When I was in Germany, our outfit had one day a year when we went to an orphanage and took kids out for a day. We took them for rides in the personnel carriers, took them to see a movie and to lunch. In general, we gave them a day like they would not have the rest of the year. I was teamed up with an eight-year-old girl. I couldn't speak German, and she couldn't speak English, but when she held my hand and looked up at me and smiled, she owned a piece of my heart. I still pray for her.

I wrote Sandy a letter about this day. You may think I was being mean, and when I see the effect it had on her, maybe I was. I was just trying to be funny. I told her I went out with this pretty girl. I had dinner with her, took her to the movies, and let her sit on my lap. "We had a pretty nice time." I wrote, "But you don't have anything to worry about because she was only eight years old." Sandy said as she started reading the letter, tears came to her eyes, and she started wondering how she was going to send her engagement ring back to me. Soon she read that the girl was only eight years old. Then she didn't want to send the ring back but just shoot me. When I look back, it wasn't as funny as I thought, and I am sorry I wrote that letter the way I did because I never wanted to bring Sandy to tears.

CHAPTER 3

I was discharged from the service on September of 1963. I went back to Thompson's Cabinet Company to get my old job back. However, I was told they didn't have a job for me at that time. I needed a job because Sandy and I were planning on getting married in October. A friend told us that Lakeside Printing was looking for a person. I applied for the job, but that was a mistake. Usually printers are given five-year apprenticeship to learn the trade. The owner said he would teach me in two weeks all there was to know. I tried, but the harder I tried, the more frustrated I got. After working there awhile, I felt I had a good idea of what hell was going to be like. My wife's aunt told us Straits Steel and Wire was hiring. I applied in the morning and went to work in the afternoon. That ended my first and only time in hell.

While working at Lakeside Printing, Sandy and I were married. This was the second best thing I ever did. The first was giving my life to Jesus, but that didn't happen for a while.

Sandy grew up in the Bethany Methodist Church, and that is where we attended church. We were married there also. After we attended there for some time, it closed its doors. We decided to go to the First Methodist Church. When more members from Bethany came over to the First Church, the name was changed to the United Methodist Church. After attending the United Methodist Church for a while, they gave me the job of head usher. I was also teaching Sunday school.

When Sandy and I had been married for a year and four days, our first son, Bruce, was born. I was so happy because God had not only given me a wife; He also gave me a son. Four years later, God gave me another son, Paul. This completed the home I asked God for years ago. God knows how to give you the best answers to your prayers, but it's always in His time.

I believe God gave me a sense of humor. After my mom died, I used that sense of humor to keep people at arm's length. I'm not sure if it was because I didn't want anyone to know how much I was hurting. I might have felt it would make you a weakling to let people see how you felt, or maybe I felt that if I let people get close to me, they might die like my mother did; I really don't remember.

I remember one radio program we used to listen to when I was a small boy. The name of the program was *Can You Top This*. As I remember it, the emcee would tell a funny story that someone had sent in, and a contestant would tell a funny story to try and get more laughs then that story. They had a laugh meter to determine who got the most laughs, and the one who got the most laughs would win a prize. There is only one story that I remember. A man walked into a fancy fruit market on Fifth Avenue in New York and asked the clerk how much his apples were. The clerk replied, "Our apples are $12 a dozen." The man thought that was too expensive and asked him how much his bananas were. The clerk said, "Our bananas are $14 a dozen." The man couldn't believe the price. He then asked the clerk, "How much are your oranges?" The clerk said, "Our oranges are $15 a dozen." The man almost had a heart attack. He turned and started walking out of the store but stopped suddenly and walked back to the clerk and handed him a dollar bill. "What's this for?" the clerk said. The customer retorted, "I stepped on one of your grapes."

As I grew older, I liked to use that sense of humor to make people laugh. Before I became a Christian, I loved to tell dirty or off-colored stories. One night, we were in a restaurant when one of my fellow workers came into the restaurant with his wife. They sat at a table near ours. I heard him tell his wife, "He's a Sunday school teacher, but you should hear some of the stories he tells us guys." That was sort of a knife in my heart. After I accepted Jesus into my heart, I could not remember any of those stories. Not that I wanted to remember them, for I was glad that garbage was out of my life. It's like Paul wrote in Romans 12:2, "Be not conformed to this world, but be transformed by the renewing of your mind, that you may know what is that good and acceptable and perfect will of God."

I am glad for the transforming power of God and the help we get from the Holy Spirit. "Grandpa, you're silly!" my granddaughter Megan said to me one day.

"Megan, would you want me to make you laugh or cry?"

"I'd rather you make me laugh," she answered.

"I guess I am doing the right thing," I replied.

When I first started my career at Straits Steel and Wire, I worked in the production end of the shop. After a while, there was a layoff. I was told to take the layoff or go to work in the plating department. My job was to strip the defective finish off the plated parts so they could be replated. When the layoff was over, they wanted me to stay in the plating department. They told me I would not be stripping anymore, but they wanted me to train as a plating supervisor. I said I would do it. I hoped that I didn't find myself in the same problem I was in at Lakeside Printing. The first day I started training, there was a plating problem. When the problem was analyzed, it was found that the plating solution was too low in caustic soda. A drum of caustic soda was placed on the catwalk. An empty drum was also put on the catwalk. I was told to put some plating solution into the empty drum and then put some of the caustic soda in and stir. When it was mixed, I was told to put the solution back into the plating tank and start doing the same thing until all of the caustic solution was in the plating tank. My supervisor then left not telling of the safety factor. When caustic soda gets mixed with a liquid, it gets very hot. When I got the caustic soda mixed and into the plating tank, I walked down off the catwalk. As I started walking around the plating tank, I thought, *Boy, are my feet getting warm!* I looked down at my feet, and to my surprise, I had gotten caustic solution on top of my new combat boots that I had bought before I got out of the service. It ate the top of the boot away. It didn't take me long to get the boots off my feet. I was lucky; no, God had His hand on me. My feet did not get burned. It was a lesson on how dangerous working with the hazardous chemical can be when you don't know what you're doing or don't respect the danger.

Working at Straits Steel and Wire was very stressful. I was learning the plating business and dealing with the problems that come up every day. I don't think I handled them very well. Oh, I did pretty good at work, but when I got home, it didn't take much to set me off. One night, I came home after working quite late. Sandy was pregnant with our first son, Bruce. She said to me, "Honey, I have a craving for some Oreo cookies. Would you go to the store and get me some?"

I said I would and headed for the store. The store didn't have any Oreo cookies, so I got Hydrox cookies. They looked like Oreo cookies, so there couldn't be much difference. When I arrived home, Sandy informed me she hated Hydrox cookies. That was the spark that set me off. I took those cookies and threw them across the room at the waste basket. It broke the top off the waste basket. We had just bought the waste basket not long before that. It was one of the few things we had been able to buy on our own. The rest of the things we had were hand-me-downs. I looked at Sandy and saw the tears in her eyes, and I hated myself.

Another time when Bruce was a small boy, I came home from work, took off my shoes at the door because I worked in nasty chemicals, turned and started to walk, and kicked one of Bruce's toys, picked it up, and threw it across the room; it bounced off the wall—broken into two pieces. These were the people I asked God to give me to love and to be loved by. When I would have these outbursts, I would look into their eyes and see the hurt. Sometimes I might even see fear. These were the people I loved best. I knew I had to change, but the harder I tried, the more things stayed the same. After a while, I gave up. I knew I was never going to change. I was a failure as a husband and father. The only messages I heard at the United Methodist Church were church doctrine.

When I was in high school, I saw a cartoon in a magazine. There was an inmate and a guard coming out of a room. There was an electric chair in this room, and heat waves were coming up from the chair. The seat of the prisoner's pants was burned out, and he said, "That reprieve didn't come any too soon." That's how I feel about Jesus; he didn't come into my life any too soon.

We were at the bowling alley one Saturday watching our boys who were bowling on a league. Paul was happy that he was finally getting out of the "baby class" in Sunday school. That Saturday, the teacher he was going to get was sitting at the bar drinking and cursing. We decided we didn't want our son in her class. It's sort of funny, yet it is not. I was headed for hell just as much as Paul's teacher. I thought I was a good Christian; I taught Sunday school. I was head usher, and I gave four dollars when they passed the offering plate. The truth of the matter was, I had never given my heart to Jesus. The only messages I heard at the United Methodist Church were church doctrines.

My brother-in-law and sister-in-law asked us, as long as we were looking for a new church, would we give theirs a try. We said we would; the next Sunday, we attended the Free Methodist Church. Our boys liked the new church and so did Sandy and I. Like I said before, the only sermons we heard at the United Methodist Church were church doctrine. I don't believe I heard one message about Jesus. We were hearing some real sermons now. They were almost all about Jesus.

We had an evening service called the hour of inspiration where people shared songs and scripture verses that were meaningful to them. They also told that Jesus, God's son, had helped them through some difficult times. One night, after hearing one of the testimonies, a light came on, and I thought, *Maybe if this Jesus was really real, maybe He could turn my life around.* As we stood to pray, I prayed also—with no fancy words, for I didn't know how to pray. I just said, "Jesus, if you really exist, if you're not just someone these people have made up, come into my life and be that same kind of a friend to me." Years have come and gone since then, I've let Him down plenty of times, but he has never failed me even once.

I remember two Christmas stories from my days as a young man watching TV. The first was *The Fourth Wise Man.* The story told of a fourth wise man. His gift for the Christ child was precious gems. He had diamonds, rubies, and other beautiful gems. The rarest and most beautiful of all was a black pearl.

They hadn't gone far when they came upon a man who lay near death. He had been beaten and robbed. One of the wise men said, "We can't take time with him. We'll have to leave him."

34

The fourth wise man said, "You go on ahead. When I take care of this man, I will catch up with you." The three wise men went on their way, and the fourth wise man stayed and nursed the man back to health. He then went on his way.

Sometime later, the fourth wise man came to a small town. It had been several years since the three wise men had departed, and he had not caught up with them yet. As he entered the town, he heard a lot of disturbance. He knocked on the door. He wanted to find out what was going on. A woman opened the door and told him soldiers were there and were going to kill all the boy children two years and younger. She feared for her little boy's life. He asked her if she would give him a drink of water. She let him come in and gave him a drink. A knock came on her door. She hid her son behind a curtain and opened the door. The soldier in charge asked her if there were any boy children in her house. She was about to answer when her baby started crying. The soldier was about to come inside and look behind the curtain when the fourth wise man said, "There's not a boy child in here." He held out his hand with a ruby in it. The soldier took the ruby and said, "Come on, men, let's get going. There's no baby in here." After the soldiers left, the mother thanked the fourth wise man, and he also went on his way.

The winds of time blew, and thirty-three years after, he started on his search for the Christ; he arrived in Jerusalem. He was old and tired, and of all the gems he started out with, he now just had that beautiful black pearl left. Although it was noon, it was as pitch-black as midnight. On a hill outside the far wall, three crosses were standing in a pale light against the darkness. Two men were standing near him holding a young girl in their grasp. The girl broke free from them and came running up to him. She dropped to her knees and pleaded with him. "Please help me, sir," she said as she cried. "My father is very sick, and he needs me. These men are taking me as payment for his debt and are going to sell me. Please help me, sir, my father needs me." The fourth wise man thought about all the pretty gems he had when he started his quest, and now all he had was that one black pearl. He reluctantly gave it to the girl to give to her captures. Just then, the ground shook and a brick from a nearby building struck him on the head; the girl held his head in her lap as he lay dying.

He looked toward the sky and uttered his final words, "Lord, I'm sorry. I have no more gifts for you."

As he breathed his last breath, he heard a voice say to him, "As you've done it onto the least of these my children, you've done it onto me."

The second Christmas story is from the old Dragnet program. It was early Christmas Eve, Friday and Gannon were on the night watch in Los Angeles. Things were pretty quiet so far, but it was still early. The phone rang, and Joe answered it. It was a priest from one of the local parishes. It seemed he had gone outside to check something and noticed the baby Jesus was missing from their manger scene. Joe said they would be over shortly. Who would steal from the manger? Was it a prank? Was it someone who was angry with the priest for something he said or did? It was 5:00 p.m. when Friday and Gannon arrived at the parish. The first thing they did was check the manger scene. The manger still held everything but the baby Jesus. They went inside and found the priest. They asked him if he had any idea who might have taken baby Jesus. He said he didn't have the faintest idea who might have taken him; he just hoped he would be returned before the eight o'clock mass. The detective said they would check around and see if anyone knew anything. They asked several people on the street if they knew who might have taken the Christ child from the cresh, but no one seemed to know. At seven thirty, they decided they had better check back in with the priest. It was only a half hour before mass. When they arrived, the priest was standing by the manger, and there was still no baby Jesus. As they were standing near the cresh talking, a boy came up the street pulling a red wagon. As he approached them, they could see in his wagon the baby Jesus. They asked him why he had taken him. He said, "All I wanted for Christmas was a red wagon. I told the baby Jesus if He would see I got it, I would give him the first ride, and I had to keep my promise to Him."

Do we ever give God a ride in our red wagon? Do we even take time to say thank you? I don't know if either one of these two

Christmas stories are true, but I know the third one is because it happened to me.

One Saturday not long before Christmas, another fellow and I were working in the plant. There was a lot of hard sludge in the bottom of the zinc tank. We worked with long-handled racks to get under the sludge. We then brought the sludge to the top and deposited in barrels. After filling the barrels, they were shipped out to be treated. We had to bend over a catwalk to drop the sludge. One time as I was straightened, I hit my head on a chunk of angle iron. It was late in the day, so we punched out and went home. I didn't do much during that whole weekend, mostly watched TV and slept.

On Monday morning before I went to work, my sister Naomi and her family arrived from Minnesota. I didn't have time to talk to them because I had to hurry to work. At work, I was hurrying to get things ready to get the plater running. I had to analyze all the tanks and pour in chemicals if needed. As I was hurrying trying to get everything done, I thought to myself, *Boy, the lights sure are funny today.* I had no idea the blood was starting to flow in my head because of having banged my head on that angle iron on Saturday. It wasn't long, and I was getting a headache. After that, I was having a hard time getting people to understand me; I also was having a difficult time understanding them. At noon, I called my wife who also had a hard time understanding me. She said, "You had better come home!"

I replied, "No, I'll be okay. After I hung up the phone, people began realizing how bad I really was and ordered a man to drive me home.

I was met at the door by my wife and sisters Naomi and Joan. They began asking me a bunch of questions. I told them I just had a touch of the flu, and I would be okay after I lie down and rest awhile. After I laid down, I looked up and saw my two little boys standing there. I guess they were worried about their daddy. I told them I'd be okay; I only need some rest. My sister Joan told Sandy not to listen to me. "He looks just like Mom did when she died," Joan said.

That frightened Sandy, so she phoned Dr. Sutter. He asked if I had hit my head. Sandy said yes. He then told her to get me into the

Ludington Hospital right away. My sister Naomi's husband, Wally, and their son Bruce helped me to the car. As I left the house, I vomited the coffee I had earlier. I continued vomiting until it was only dry heaves. By the time I reached the hospital, I was pretty much out of it. It seemed like I was in a cloud. All of a sudden, I heard voices—the voices of Sandy and the doctor. When he realized I was awake, he asked me to squeeze his fingers. He then told Sandy it was yet too early to tell, but it might be two weeks before they would know if they have to go in and operate. He said to her, "Bruce should be taken to Hackley Hospital in Muskegon, so if surgery is necessary, he will already be there." When Sandy told me what doctor said, I replied, "Merry Christmas." I felt I would not be home to spend Christmas with my family. I said to Sandy, "He didn't want me to die on his chart. That's why he wants me to go to Muskegon." I just said that to be funny, for he's not like that at all. He's a fine caring doctor. Sandy rode with me in the ambulance as we went to Muskegon. Though she could not see, she knew I was still alive when she heard me vomit.

It was only a few days before Christmas, and Sandy didn't know how she was going to juggle Christmas between the boys in Ludington and me in Muskegon. It was hard on Sandy not knowing if I was going to live or die—a young mother with two small boys. I had three things going for me—it was a wonderful hospital and a fine brain surgeon looking after me and I had a lot of people praying for me. I'm not going to make a long story longer. In spite of the spinal tap, in spite of the liquid diet, there is a happy ending to this story. I phoned Sandy on Christmas Eve day and told her I could come home. It wasn't two weeks nor even one week after my arrival in the hospital; it was four days! I got to come home and spend Christmas with my wife and two sons. God gets the glory! Not just for the birth of his son but also for taking care of another son.

It was only a few months after the severe concussion that I got another head injury. I was working late one night trying to get caught up on my work. I needed to get some hydraulic oil for the plater. I went into the chemical room and slipped on some spilled oil. I fell backward and hit the back of my head on the rim of a fifty-five-gallon metal barrel. I felt my head and saw the blood on my hand. Thoughts race through my mind. What if I would pass out in the chemical room? I could lie here a long time before someone would find me. I ran out where some people were working. They saw me, saw my head was bleeding, and someone took me to the hospital. Dr. Sutter sewed up my head and said, "I wish you would injure something besides your head for a change."

Before I became a Christian, I would always say the pastor said the Bible says this or the Bible says that. After I accepted Jesus, I no longer was content to take the pastor's word for what the Bible said. Not that I thought the pastor would lie to me, but I just had to find out for myself. I would come home from work and get a shower, eat supper, get my Bible, and head to the bedroom to read the Bible and spend time with Jesus. One day, Sandy said to me that I just wasn't spending enough time with her and the boys. She was right. I was spending most of my time with Jesus and neglecting her and the boys. It was a tough problem. I think God gave the only true solution. I started getting up an hour early and spending time with Jesus. In the evening, I would spend time with Sandy and the boys.

4
CHAPTER

The Thompson family was a special family in the Ludington Free Methodist Church. The family consisted of Lynn; his wife, Christine; and two daughters, Sherry and Dawn. They would go all over the city on Wednesday nights picking up kids and bring them to church. There wasn't anything they wouldn't do for anyone.

One summer early in my Christian walk, we took a vacation with the Thompson family. We stopped at Lynn's brother's house near Jackson for a while. We then went to Cedar Point and on to Sea World. We had a blast!

I looked up to Lynn, not because he was taller, but I knew in my heart he was the man God was proud of. One day God spoke to me; He could have said, "Bruce, you're supposed to try and be like Me. I'm the one who is perfect." God could have, but He didn't. Instead, He said, "You'll never be the Bruce Wright original I created you to be as long as you're trying to be a counterfeit of Lynn Thompson."

Lynn's name pops up in my life every so often. One time it didn't start with Lynn. It all started on a normal Friday morning at work. I was analyzing the solutions in different tanks on the plater. The cleaner tank needed more cleaner, this tank held alkaline. The PH scale is simple. Neutral PH is 7. Going below 7 is acid, above 7 is alkaline. Alkaline will burn just like acid will. I looked for the metal pail I used to pour the cleaner into the tank. I couldn't find it, so I used a cardboard zinc ball container. I filled it with cleaner and went up the catwalk to put the cleaner in the tank. The cleaner must be poured into the tank very slowly because the cleaner tank was at the boiling point. If the cleaner is put in too fast, it will boil over. I was in a hurry and had not realized the cardboard container had been setting in water. As I started sprinkling the cleaner into the tank, the bottom fell out of the cardboard container. Suddenly, the entire cleaner dropped into the tank—all at once. I knew what was coming, and all I could do was to lean against the railing and wait to get hit with the blast of boiling cleaner. I didn't have long to wait! I was hit with the boiling hot cleaner from my neck down past my stomach. I never wore a belt, but that day, I was wearing one. I guess I was lucky because the belt kept the cleaner from running further down my body. You could say "luck," but I don't believe in luck. I believe the Holy Spirit laid it on me to wear a belt that day.

Some of the suds from the cleaner got into my hair, and some hair fell into my eye. I was taken to Dr. Sutter's office. Because I got some in my eye, he sent me to the eye doctor first. That doctor rinsed out my eye and put drops in it. He put a patch over the eye and sent me back to Dr. Sutter who rinsed the alkaline off my body and neutralized it. He gave me a pain pill and sent me home.

I tried to get comfortable but couldn't! I had rolls of blisters, and it was too painful to sit. I didn't sleep much that night either. The next morning, Lynn Thompson came to the house; he had come to pray with me. "Bruce, we are going to pray that God heals you and that you don't even have a tiny scar left."

"No, Lynn, I'm going to pray that I have one tiny scar so I will never forget who healed me." Today, so many years later, I have one tiny scar at the corner of my arm pit.

Some years back when I was giving God credit for healing me, suddenly Satan said to me, "Bruce, you're stupid. That was just a natural body healing."

"Satan, you're just as big a liar as you ever were—and here's the proof!" I said as I touch that little scar.

When God told Moses He wanted him to lead His people out of Egypt, Moses said to God, "What if the people ask who has sent me and I tell them the God of their fathers have sent me. What if they ask what His name is? What should I tell them?"

"Tell them 'I AM' has sent you."

In the New Testament, Jesus said "I Am" several times.

John 6:35: I Am the bread of life.
John 8:12: I Am the light of the world
John 10:9: I Am the gate.
John 10:11: I Am the good shepherd.
John 10:36: I Am God's Son.
John 11:25: I Am the resurrection.
John 14:6: I Am the way, the truth, and the life.
John 15:11: Am the true vine.

I Am is like a blank check. I Am able to meet all your needs. Just fill in the amount, and you can take it to the bank and cash it, because I Am's bank account never runs out.

I have always backed all of the pastors we have had over the years. They are put here by God. If I were to go up against them, I would be going against God. After a few years at the Free Methodist Church, we got a new pastor. I loved him and his wife, but we no longer had the Sunday night hour of inspiration. He picked out a couple of songs to sing and preached a short message, and then we went home. I was devastated! I was saved in the hour of inspiration service, and now it is over. I decided to try other churches on Sunday evening but couldn't do it without God's okay. I said, "God if it's okay for us to try other churches next Sunday, let us have the same kind of service we've been having here at home."

The next Sunday, we went to Grand Rapids to visit Sandy's sister and her family. We went to a Baptist Church. When the pastor started to give his sermon, the first words out of his mouth were "Why did you come this morning? Is it to worship God or for what you can get out of it"? I wondered how he knew I was there. I looked around and didn't see anyone I knew. "Okay, God, I understand what you're saying," I said later that day. I never again thought about leaving that church. I believe I've always been a part of God's plan for this church.

When the boys were little, I was a young Christian even though I was in my thirties. I would always get up early and could hardly wait to get to church. There was one thing I couldn't understand. Sandy had been a Christian all her life, yet she would say, "I hate Sundays." It sorts of reminded me of the movie *Pollyanna*. Pollyanna was the daughter of missionaries who were killed. She had to go live with her aunt Polly. Aunt Polly was rich and pretty much ran the town. She even told the pastor what to preach, and it was always hell fire and damnation. When he spoke, the chandeliers would shake. One Sunday after church, Pollyanna was in the kitchen with some of the servants. They were fixing chicken for dinner and grumbling. Pollyanna always played a glad game. She always found something to be glad about.

One of the servants said, "I hate Sundays. We go to church and hear the same message and then come home and have chicken. I hate Sundays."

Pollyanna said, "You need to play the glad game." The servant said to Pollyanna, "Okay, Ms. Goody Two-Shoes, what can you find glad about Sunday?"

Pollyanna thought awhile and said, "Well, you can be glad because it will be seven days before it comes again." I decided I was going to have to teach Sandy the glad game.

The Holy Spirit interrupted and said, "Bruce, don't you think the reason Sandy doesn't have the same attitude as you do is because she has three people to get ready for church and you only have one?" After that, I began helping Sandy get the boys ready for church, and she started enjoying Sunday too.

"Bruce, I want you to begin tithing," God said to me one day.

"But, Lord, that's what we're working at. When I came to the Free Methodist Church, we were giving ten dollars. Now we are giving fifteen. As we can, we'll keep giving more until we reach a tithe."

"No," God said, "I want you to tithe now."

I didn't argue with Him, but I didn't do what He asked me to do. For the next period, I felt God was neglecting me. He wasn't talking to me anymore. It was the coldest, deadest time I've experienced as a Christian. Finally, when I couldn't stand it anymore, I said to Him, "Lord, how come you're not talking to me anymore?" I don't know if I was trying to con God or not. I think I knew down deep in my heart the answer to my own question.

God answered me, "Bruce, you know why I'm not talking to you. I asked you to do something, and you are not doing it. There's nothing more to talk about."

I knew I couldn't go on like I was. I told God I would tithe. Now I had to convince Sandy. She had asked me before to give more money, but I said no. I felt, "Why should I give money to people who had more money than I did?" It seemed everyone had to be paid for everything they did. You can tell I wasn't a Christian back then. Sandy didn't greet my message with tears of joy. We were struggling to make ends meet. One of her comments was what if the boys needed a new pair of shoes. The only thing I could say was "God will provide." I don't think in my Christian walk right then that I really believed my own statement. If I had been a mature Christian, I would have known God just wants us to learn to trust Him. For some time, it was difficult to tithe. I think it was because we did it because God wanted us to, not because we wanted to tithe to please God. Sometime later, it became a joy to tithe. We saw we already had enough. Sometimes people would give us food out of their gardens. Sometimes I would work overtime. It became a joy looking forward to see how God was going to meet our needs this next time.

I went to work one day as usual, but it turned out to be anything but usual. About halfway through the morning, the conveyor belt stopped. I checked one gearbox, and it seemed okay. As I checked the other gearbox, I discovered the chain bound up. I looked all over for a ladder but could not find one anywhere. But I saw a fifty-five-gallon drum, moved it into position, and climbed onto it so I could reach the gearbox. I freed the chain, but one of the links was bent. I changed that link and jumped down from the barrel. However, my feet never hit the floor. My wedding ring became caught on a piece of the flat steel, and there I hung. It seemed like I was hanging there quite a while, though it was only a few seconds. I suddenly felt my flesh on my finger tear, and I dropped to the floor. I looked at my hand and didn't like what I saw—my ring was hidden beneath the flesh of my finger. I was taken to the hospital where the doctor cut off my ring before stitching my torn finger. Most injuries like this one would mean the loss of a finger. That is why I say God has given me eleven fingers. The ten original fingers, plus the one I didn't lose.

Another day at work, I was busy trying to get my work caught up. I was putting zinc balls into the zinc ball baskets. I got one side of the plater loaded and took a container of about fifty pounds of zinc round to the other side of the plater. I had to take those zinc balls up a ladder to get on the catwalk, which was about five feet off the floor. The ladder was a metal rung ladder that had a loop at the top. The looped ends fit in holes in the catwalk to hold the ladder in place. I started climbing up the ladder, but the ladder came out of the catwalk, and I fell backward from about four feet high and landed on my back on the concrete floor. I laid there with the fifty pounds of zinc balls on my chest. I struggled trying to get the zinc balls off my chest so I could get up.

Roger Geroscy came over and looked down at me. Roger was about twenty cards short of playing with a full deck. I thought Roger had come over to help me up, but he just laughed and said, "Ha, ha, that was funny, Bruce. You want to do it again?" As I struggled to get the zinc balls off my chest, my thoughts were of wrapping my fingers around Roger's neck and squeezing. I finally got the zinc bails off my chest, and I had cooled down a little by then realizing that Roger was Roger. He probably didn't even think that I might have been hurt.

As I look back on that day, it's kind of funny now, but back then, it was far from being funny. The last thing I am going to tell you about that day is the only real damage was to my pride.

One Sunday morning, the pastor was gone, and our lay minister had the service. He had spoken several times earlier. It seemed that he didn't prepare much. On his behalf, he was a businessman and probably didn't have much time to prepare. He mainly spoke about the "good ole days" in the Free Methodist Church. I felt God deserves our best and not our leftovers. I made a comment about the fact that I would've loved to hear him preach. A saint of the church heard me and said to me, "Bruce, why don't you study and become a lay minister? I'll buy the books." I said I would. Even though he asked me in a nice way, what I think he was really saying was, "If you think it's so easy, let's see if you can do better." He did buy my books for the first year. After that, I paid for my own books. I guess I felt guilty about finding fault with another Christian.

The Bible says in 1 Corinthians 13:7 in the Living Bible, "If you love someone, you will be loyal to him no matter what the cost. You always believe in him, always expect the best in him, and always stand your ground in defending him."

Boy, did I blow that one! But God, in all His mercy, still allowed me to become a lay minister. I know that sometimes I probably put some people to sleep, but I tried to always give God my best. I know we aren't supposed to be prideful, but I think one of my proudest moments as a lay minister was when I helped baptize my grand-daughter Sierra.

5
CHAPTER

I was never a boy scout when I was young. I guess my main interest was baseball and football. When my son Bruce was young, he wanted to be in cub scouts. There was only one problem—there was no cub master. I was asked to be their cub master, but I really didn't want to do it. After so many excuses, I stepped out of my comfort zone and became the cub master. I remained cub master as long as Bruce and Paul were in cub scouts.

I then followed them to boy scouts. Every year, I took a week's vacation so I could go to Camp Gerber with the boys. Bruce became an Eagle Scout and also earned a God and Country Award. Paul was one merit badge and his Eagle project from earning his Eagle rank. They both did really well in scouting. I would like to think my involvement in scouting helped them along the scouting trail.

If I had a moment in scouting that has really stuck with me, it was at Camp Gerber. A scout named Duane Brewer was away from home for the first time. His brother Charles and his friends didn't make it any easier for him. They seemed to take delight in teasing him. Duane wasn't signed up for many classes, but he enjoyed the rifle range. They had a time every day that they could pay a dime and shoot. The highest scores got prizes. One day, the instructor told the boys that the final boy had fired, and he would add up the scores. As he read off the scores, he overlooked Duane's scores. Duane went hyper! He accused the instructor of cheating him out of his dime. Duane kicked over the trash can and stormed off the rifle range in tears. The instructor felt bad and wanted to find Duane and give him his dime back. I told the instructor I would handle this. I first picked up the trash and then went to the campsite. I didn't see anyone in camp, but I noticed Duane's tent was doing a lot of moving. I knew he was inside. Duane was still upset. I told him to settle down. "He cheated me out of my dime," Duane cried.

"Oh no, Duane," I said. "Nobody is here to cheat you. They are here to see that you kids have a good time. It was just an oversight." I reached into my pocket and took out a dime and reached it to him, but as he reached to get it, the dime fell to the floor and through a crack in the floor, out of reach. I handed him another dime; this time, he secured it.

"Duane, what do you want to do now?" I asked him, hoping to continue calming him.

"I wanna go to the lake."

"Can you swim?" I asked as we walked along.

"No."

Every Boy Scout must pass the swimming merit badge, so I got him signed up for swimming lessons during the rest of the week. Duane became a happy camper after that.

Wednesday night was family night at camp. Duane was walking with his mother and father and introduced me to them.

"Mr. Wright are you going to be here all week?" he asked.

"Yes, I am."

"Decent!" he said. I guess I had made a difference for Duane. Instead of going home with his mom and dad on Wednesday, he stayed at camp all week, and besides learning to swim, he did many other things. Duane also earned several merit badges. I guess the only way I could have helped Duane more would have been if I would have introduced him to Jesus, but alas, I didn't know Jesus myself then.

There is a day in my memory that if God had not had his hand on me, I would not be writing this story today. That day started just like most days. I went to work a little early so I could see how things went on the third shift just hours earlier. After talking to the third shift foreman, I decided everything was okay, and I could check the waste treatment. As I entered the waste treatment, I noticed the chlorinator was not working. We used chlorine gas to treat cyanide. We obtained the gas in four-thousand-pound tanks. I placed the chlorinator in the big tank so I could determine how much chlorine was dispensed into the tank. Then I placed the chlorine tank on a scale to measure the amount of chlorine remaining in the tank. The gauge showed there was still a few hundred pounds of chlorine gas remaining. I decided the few hundred the low amount of chlorine in the tank had to be the cause of the chlorinator not working.

When a bad decision is made, it can sometimes be deadly. This time, two bad decisions were made. The first bad decision was discovered when I reached for the key to get the respirator and discovered it was missing. I guess they thought it might get stolen. When you work around hazardous chemicals, it's smart to wear a respirator. Bad decision number two: I decided I needed to get the chlorine gas going into the cyanide waste tank—respirator or not. No telling how long chlorine gas was not being pumped into the cyanide waste tank. There would be time to analyze the tank once I got the chlorine pumping into it. I shut the valve off on the chlorine. It must have been a bad valve; when I took the chlorinator off the tank, the chlorine gas came gushing out. I held my breath and tried to screw the cap on the tank to stop the chlorine. I was too shaky from not breathing. I ran as far away as I could and took a deep breath. I ran back to the tank and tried once again to get the valve on the tank, but I couldn't. I was shaking too much from the lack of oxygen.

A voice said to me, "Get out of here. You had too much gas already." I knew it must have been God speaking to me. I went back into the plating department and headed for the office. When I arrived in the office, the secretary asked me what was wrong. I couldn't answer her; all I could do was cough. When you inhale chlorine gas, it lies in the bottom of the lungs and causes you to cough. The secretary called the president of the company. He came down from his office and said he knew where I had been because I smelled like his swimming pool. He asked the secretary to take me to the hospital, but she said no, she couldn't. She had a son who died in her arms, and she was afraid I would also die. The president drove me to the hospital. They put me on oxygen and started doing tests. This was the only time in my adult life I didn't know if I was going to live or die. I remember God had told me I had too much chlorine gas, so I knew my life was in His hands. By the time I was wheeled into the intensive care unit, I had God's assurance I was going to make it. Sandy said when she and her dad arrived, they still didn't think I was going to make it. Just then the nurse brought some whiskey. "I don't want any whiskey."

"Take it, honey, its medicine," Sandy urged. Whiskey was used as a medicine to keep the lungs from drying out. I still didn't want it because God brought me through the time of not knowing if I was going to live or die, and I wasn't going to trust whiskey to bring me through the rest of the way. The next day, God showed me he approved of not trusting whiskey instead of Him.

There were seven other people who got a sniff of chlorine at the plant. They were all in a ward. I was in ICU. The doctor looked them over and released them. He then came up to the intensive care unit and released me. When I got to the nurse's station, the last of the seven men was getting wheeled to the elevator to go home. "There are no more wheelchairs. We could either wait for a wheelchair to be returned or she could walk to the car with me," the nurse said.

"Let's walk!" I said.

The Lord showed me something: the men who weren't very bad off got wheeled down like they were the ones at death's door. The one who was at death's door walked out of the hospital like a visitor.

I told this story to one of my pastors, and he said to me, "That was against the law. God couldn't do that."

"God can do whatever he wants to. He makes the laws," I told him.

A short time ago, I had a chest X-ray that showed what could be scar tissue. It could have been caused from when I smoked in my younger day, or it could have been from the chlorine gas. Sandy said, "The scars are because you didn't drink the whiskey."

I said, "Oh no, it was just another reminder of whose hands I'm in."

Another time, we were on our way to Manistee one Sunday afternoon. We were about two-thirds of the way when a car coming toward us passed another car. He was headed right at us. The only thing we could do was to head for the shoulder of the road. We were able to get to the side of the road. Once we got by him, we came back on the highway. After we quit shaking, we began to talk.

"I don't remember that there was a shoulder big enough for a car to ride on," Sandy agreed. Then we planned to look carefully as we drove back home. It had snowed, so we had a harder time finding the exact spot. When we got to the area, we started looking for tracks where we ran off the highway. We never found enough of a shoulder where we could have gone off. The only possible solution we could think of was that God had his angels pick up our car and carry us off and back onto the highway. Praise God for His protection.

One morning, I came into work early as usual. One other person also came in early. That person loaded the plater while I got the chemicals into the machine. I had just memorized Romans 8:35–39. It says,

> "Who shall separate us from the love of Christ? Shall tribulation, or distress, or persecution, or famine, or nakedness, or peril or sword?
>
> As it is written, for thy sake we are killed all the day long; we are accounted as sheep for the slaughter. Nay, in all these things we are more than conquerors through him that loved us. For I am persuaded, that neither death, nor life, nor angels, nor principalities, nor powers, nor things present, nor things to come, not heights, not depth, nor any other creature, shall be able to separate us from the love of God, which is in Christ Jesus our Lord.

I recited it for my coworker. That person said, "That's amazing."

I said, "It's not amazing that I memorized that. What's amazing is there is nothing or nobody that can separate us from God's love." For a non-Christian, his response blew my mind. The response was "only us." That tells me even non-Christians realize that God has done all He can do by allowing his Son to go to the cross for us. Whether we except His free gift or not is our choice.

I once told a fellow Christian that prayerlessness is a sin. She told me, "Oh no, it is not." I wonder how she would feel if her kids came into her house and ate her food, slept in her bed, and took a shower in her bathroom and never took time to spend with her. I wonder how she would feel.

I wonder what she would do if she found herself in a situation she couldn't figure out. I wonder if she would worry about it or say to God, "Daddy, I have a problem." She would probably worry about it first and then pray. Sometimes we get ourselves so uptight about this, that, or the other thing, that we can make ourselves sick with worry.

Philippians 4:6–8 tells us not to worry about anything but to pray about everything. Isn't that good advice from God?

God doesn't want us to worry; he wants us to trust him. Worry is a burden that God never wanted us to bear. Wouldn't it be smarter to trust the one who created us rather than to worry about anything?

I like this line from *Our Daily Bread* devotional. It says, "Courage is fear that has said its prayers."

Another line from *Our Daily Bread* is, "When we put our problems in God's hands, He puts His peace in our hearts." What a wonderful God we serve.

Sandy and I became involved in the children's group in our church called Christian Life Crusaders (CLC) that met every Wednesday evening. Sandy taught kindergarten through third grade, and I taught fourth grade through sixth. Earning a John Wesley Medallion was the goal of every kid in my group. The requirement to gain that reward was to memorize Ephesians 6:10–17. That took a lot of work. Doreen Dwyer and Paul Wright were the only ones to earn that award from our church.

One night, I only had Sandy Dwyer in my class. When I told her it was time to work on her memory verse, she said, "I don't know why I should have to learn it. You don't know it."

That was like a knife going through my heart. I might have blown that off, but God also spoke to me, saying, "Bruce, she's right you know. You expect these children to learn their verses, and you don't know them. You're a hypocrite!"

That even hurt more. If a person tells you something like that, you can say, "What do you know?" But when God tells you, you have to listen. God can't lie. I decided I had better learn that scripture, and I did. I continued memorizing scripture. Today I am getting close to having three hundred scriptures memorized. Some people say memorizing scripture is hard, but it is not; it is hard when you don't try. While I was memorizing a Bible verse, Sandy would give me the address of the verse (where it is located in the Bible), and I would quote the verse. After I learned so many, Sandy told me she didn't have time to practice with me that way. I knew them, so I quit going over them.

One day a television pastor mentioned memory verses. I wondered if I still knew the ones I had memorized during the time Sandy would drill me and was surprised how many I had forgotten.

The Lord spoke to me, "If you will learn those verses again, Bruce, I will show you how to keep them."

I worked hard and learned them. Then the Lord continued his teaching, "Bruce, write the verses on three by five cards and go over some of the cards every day. Those that you review can be put on the bottom of the stack. After so many days, you will have gone over all of them."

My favorite is Zephaniah 3:17. I love all the scriptures, but this one is my favorite because God spoke to me through this verse. It says:

> The Lord your God is with you.
> He is mighty to save. He will take great delight
> in you.
> He will quiet you with His love.
> He will rejoice over you with singing.

That blew my mind; I never thought of God as singing. I memorized that verse and thought about it quite a lot.

6
CHAPTER

Sandy and I came home from church on Sunday, and she went into the kitchen to fix lunch and was singing, as she always did. God spoke to me.

"Bruce, Sandy is out in the kitchen fixing your lunch, not because she is married to you and she has to. She is doing it because she loves you, and that's why she is singing. It's the same with me. I created you, and I take care of you daily—not because I created you and I have to. I take care of you because I love you, and that's why I'm singing."

If that doesn't thrill your heart, I don't know what will! That God who created over 350 billion galaxies loves you so much he takes care of you every day.

One day, I asked God, "Lord, why did you give me a love for music and never gave me a singing voice?" He didn't answer me, but he gave me two memories from the past. The first memory was about my childhood friend Gary. He and I found a large cardboard box from somewhere. We dragged it home and set it up on our porch and climbed up on it pretending we were riding a stagecoach. My sister Joan came along and asked what we were doing. Gary told her we were riding a stagecoach. "Can I come up there with you?" she asked. "Sure," was the answer. She climbed on the box when suddenly it caved in. We were all on the ground laughing and laughing. We weren't hurt but sure must have thought it was funny.

My second memory was about my sisters and me. I was singing a song and kept changing the words. For some reason, this irritated my sisters. They cried out to my mom to make me stop. I thought

I would probably get the "ruler of correction," but Mom just said, "Leave him alone. How do you think song writers write songs?"

I don't know what happened next, but being the little brat I was, I probably kept on annoying my sisters.

When God first began giving me songs, He would give me both tunes and words. All I had to do then was put them on paper. This seemed pretty neat to me considering I don't have a musical bone in my body. God let me know though that as soon as I took credit for just one of these songs, He would never give me another.

This next story shows how God works. One Wednesday, I had a very bad cough. I couldn't get into the doctor until Friday. By the time I saw him, I was so bad I thought I was going to die. The doctor said I had bronchitis and gave me some medicine. I went to bed quite early that night. Saturday morning, I woke up about 3:00 feeling so much better. All of a sudden, I jumped out of bed. That woke up Sandy who wanted to know what was going on. I told her everything was okay and that God was giving me a song, and I had to get a pencil and paper to write it down. Following is that song:

Step by Step I'm In My Father's Care

Chorus

Step by step I feel my Father guide me
Step by step is all I ever need,
Step by step I feel His love around me,
Step by step I'm in my Father's care
Satan's evil war he wages
Against everyone he sees
But his fiery darts can't harm me
For my Father's love envelopes me.

Chorus

Satan cause men to hurt us
And our pain is in his grip

But our Father's law is in us
And His love is on our lips

Chorus

When life's trials and temptations
Are all that I can see
They will never overcome me
For my Father walks with me

Chorus

Step by step I feel my Father guide me,
Step by step is all I ever need,
Step by step I feel His love around me,
Step by step I'm in my Father's care
Step by step I feel His love around me,
Step by step I'm in my Father's care

Sandy and I had the tradition of going out on our wedding anniversary. This one-year thing changed. It was our thirtieth anniversary; I had to work. We were shutting down the plating division in the plant, and I had to be there. I called Sandy at noon and told her how bad I felt. She said she understood and it was okay. After I hung up the phone, I still felt bad, so I asked God to help me write something to let Sandy know how I felt. Within fifteen minutes, I called Sandy and told her the poem God had given me for her.

God Made
God made Jupiter and God made Mars,
God made Venus and God made the stars,
God made the mountains and God made the hills,
God made the roses and God made the daffodils,
God made the mists and God made the fogs,
God made the camel and God made the razor-
    back hog,

God made the pheasant to all to see,
But, honey, God made you just for me.

Sandy loved this poem, and I did too. It was the best anniversary present I could have given her because it came from the Lord. Thanks again, Father.

Many years later, I was taking a shower. I was enjoying the nice hot water running on me. I started praising God for all he had done for me. I praised him for giving me life, I praised him for giving me new life in Jesus, I praised him for giving me my wife, Sandy, I praised him for giving me my two boys, I praised him for my five grandchildren, I praised him for the songs he had given me, and I praised him for the poem he had given me. God stopped me and said, "Who told you that was a poem? I didn't." That poem came quite a while before "Come on Jesus," which I thought was my first song God had given me. He always gave me the tune first, so I was surprised when he told me it was a song not a poem and to go ahead and sing it. I did as he told me and sang it. God was right as always; it was a song. God has a way that every once and a while he lets us know, in a loving way, that we don't know quite as much as we think we do.

In 1 Corinthians 8:1–3, it says, "We know that we possess knowledge. Knowledge puffs up, but love builds up. The man who thinks he knows something, does not yet know as he ought to know. But the man who loves God is known by God." Thank You, Father, for letting us know sometimes that we aren't as smart as we think we are.

Sometime later, I put my mouth in action before my brain got in gear. I said something that I shouldn't have said. I don't remember what I said, but Sandy wasn't happy with me. There wasn't anything I could say or do to make Sandy or me feel better. I had to depend on the one who always bails me out. I said, "Lord, help me write another song so Sandy will know how sorry I am for what I said." God gave me the song "I Love You."

I Love You
I love you in the morning before I start to pray
I love you in the evening at the close of every day

I love you in the springtime when the winter cold
    is done.
I love you in the summer when the warmth of
    the sun has come
I love you in the fall when the harvest crops are
    for sale
I love you in the winter when its strong winds
    do prevail
I love you when I see you, my heart skips a beat
I want to hold and kiss you, our love is oh so sweet
And honey, I still love you even though we're
    growing old
And I will always love you, my love will not grow
    cold
My love for you is forever, what more is there to say
I need you here beside me each and every day

I could never write anything like this, because I am not a writer. God helps me write all the things I write, even *To God Be the Glory*. God tells us to ask, and we shall receive that our joy may be full. It is not that we deserve it, but it is that he loves us, and he wants us to be happy.

I don't pray anymore asking God why he gave me a love for music but never gave me a singing voice. Although he didn't answer me, I think he gave me the answer I needed. If he had given me a singing voice when I was younger, I wasn't a Christian yet, so my singing voice would have been used to glorify myself and not God. When I think about that, I am glad I don't have a singing voice. All these years have gone by, and God has given me something more precious; he gave me all these songs. Although he's given me all these songs, I can't complete them by putting notes to them. I just have no musical ability whatsoever. I have prayed for some time for God to send someone to put notes to them for me.

Our church had lost a lot of our members and needed help to try and get on track. A pastor we once had brought his praise band and came up on Saturday nights. He hoped to stir interest in some of those that had left to come back.

One night two of the men in the praise band sang a song one of them had written. It was beautiful. After the service, I asked the one that had written it if he had put notes to it. He said no, the other man had. I told the other man, whose name was Brad, that God had given me several songs. I said the only problem was I didn't have any notes for them. Brad said if I would put some of them on a tape, he would put notes to them. He said he would be busy for the next couple months, but he could do it after that. Two weeks later, he brought one of the songs he had put notes to. I was *overjoyed*.

The praise band and the pastor haven't been back. That one song is still the only one I have notes for. I still pray for someone to come and put notes to the rest of them. I won't stop praying for someone to put notes to the rest of them. They are good songs, and they give God honor and glory.

I don't want you to think that I am not grateful for the one song that now has notes. I am very grateful, and I love it dearly, but I want to share with you something God has taught me. Always be thankful for what you have instead of complaining about what you don't have. With this attitude, you give God honor and Glory.

The man (Brad) who wrote notes to the first song, quite a while after he wrote notes to the first song, sent the other five songs back in the mail. They also had notes written to them. I was tickled pink. I gave Brad a big thank you. I only have twenty-seven songs left at this time without notes. You also earned a big thank you, Jesus.

There was only one more time I asked God to help me write anything besides what I'm writing now. Sandy's mother had a stroke. She had to go into a nursing home. Sandy, being the good daughter she was, went to the nursing home every day; at first, two times a day. When this got to be too much, Sandy cut it back, and her mother understood. Sandy was a faithful daughter visiting her mother in the nursing home for six years. When her mother died, Sandy went through a period of mourning. I don't think Sandy thought she was, but I do. I didn't really recognize it either. I don't think that I really was the comfort and support I should have been. Sandy had always been a wonderful daughter. She helped her parents every time they needed help. Now she needed someone to help her through this hard time of loss, and I missed the boat. She let me know it too! I can't tell you how she let me now, but it was just one of those things you know. I felt bad. Sandy had always been there for me, and now I let her down. I asked God to help me write a song for Sandy so she would know how I felt deep down in my heart. God answered my prayer and gave me this song:

Special Angel

You are my Special angel, God sent you from above
To give me so much happiness, to fill my life
with love,
And I thank the Lord above for giving you to me.
You are my Special Angel; you mean the world
to me.
You are my Special Angel: I love you more each day,
I love you with a love so true, more than words
can say,
And I thank the Lord above for giving you to me.
You are my Special Angel, you mean all the world
to me.
You are my Special Angel; our love was meant
to be.
We'll walk hand and hand through all eternity.
And I thank the Lord above for giving you to me.
You are my Special Angel, you mean the world
to me.
And I thank the Lord above for giving you to me.
You'll be my Special Angel throughout eternity.

Sandy loves her song. It was another great job by the Lord. He bailed me out of another poor job. Thanks again, Lord.

When my son Paul got married, I got myself into another fine mess. I wasn't feeling good that weekend, but I still wanted this to be a special weekend for him. I made it through the wedding and the reception on Saturday. The following day was Sunday. I wasn't feeling any better. In the afternoon, after church, we went up to Stronach where the reception had taken place. My daughter-in-law's family traditionally returned to the reception hall on the following day to clean the hall. The bride and groom opened their gifts at this time. I loaded the car with all the things that were to go back home. The car was full. I swept the floor, and because I wasn't feeling good, I went to the car and sat down. Soon the best man and an usher came to the car with a five-gallon bucket of mashed potatoes and two pots of flowers. They said, "Sandy's sister told us to put these in the car."

"What am I supposed to do with them?" I snapped.

"Am I supposed to hold a pot in each hand and sit in the bucket of mashed potatoes?" They didn't know what to say, so they just stood there. I got out of the car and said, "I'll take care of them."

I went back inside and told Sandy who was sympathetic and said, "Cool your jets!"

I fired back. "I'll cool my jets! I'll walk home!" I stormed out the door and headed down the road. It was not a very smart thing to do. I wasn't feeling well, I had dress shoes on, it would be a twenty-five-mile walk, and furthermore, I wasn't sure where home was.

I remembered when we came, we drove down a hill. The first hill I saw, I walked to the top. When I got there, I headed to the west for a while. I knew this was not the hill we came down. I thought, *If I go back, I might be more lost.* I knew if I'd keep going west, I'd still be going toward home. The more I walked, the worse I felt. When I heard a car coming up behind me, I'd say to myself, "They finally found me." As the car passed me, I'd think, "If they really loved me, they would be looking for me." I got myself into a mess and now was feeling sorry for myself. The truth of the matter was—Sandy and Paul were both driving around looking for me. They looked everywhere but on the road where I was. I guess they thought I wouldn't be dumb enough to take that road. I sure proved them wrong!

I kept walking and feeling bad. I finally said, "Lord, I'm lost. I could surely use your help." Just then, I looked way up the road on the horizon and saw a speck going from one side of the road to the other. I wasn't sure if it was an animal or a person. As the speck grew closer, I could see it was a man. A friend of mine later told me he was probably looking for beer cans to turn in for money. When I got close enough to him, I asked, "Sir, can you tell me which way is the highway?"

He pointed down the road and said, "When you get to that next corner turn right, and it will lead you right to the highway." It seemed forever before I got to that corner. As I arrived there, I thought to myself, *If I turn right, I'll be going back toward Manistee.*

A voice said to me, "If you didn't want directions, why did you ask for them?" I decided that was the Lord speaking to me. I was smart enough to know when the Lord speaks, I should listen. I turned right, and before long, I could see cars speeding along the highway. I turned left on that road and began walking south.

I had not walked far when I could see a billboard. Soon I could read the words, and I wanted to cry. The words said, "Nineteen miles to Ramada Inn." Home was five miles beyond that. I said, "Lord, I'm tired, I'm sick, and you know I'll never make it." I had not walked far when I saw a car turning around and coming back toward me. It was the brother of Paul's best man.

Tommy asked, "Mr. Wright, do you need a ride?" He took me all the way home. When I got inside, I phoned Paul at his hotel room and told him I was sorry. I wanted this to be a weekend he'd never forget.

He said, "Dad, you can be sure I'll never forget this weekend!" Sometime later, Paul and I drove to Manistee. On the way back, we traced my steps to see how far I had walked that day. It was almost eight miles. I could never have survived if God had not helped me. The old adage that God protects the innocent and the ignorant applies to me many times.

Sometime later, Paul invited Sandy and me to go with them to Disney World in Florida. We accepted the offer and joined the group. There were Paul and Gina, Megan, Sierra, Gina's mother and dad, Gina's brother and wife and two children, Gina's grandmother and her boyfriend. We drove to the Detroit airport. Before we could board the airplane, we had to be checked. All our metal objects had to be placed in a pan, and then they check us with a metal detector. I had a knee replacement and had a card that said that, but they wouldn't accept it. I had to get screened like everyone else. For some reason, I had my driver's license out. When I was getting checked, I put it in my shirt pocket. The buzzer went off when they went over my knee. It also went off when they went over my pocket. I didn't think it should have gone off; there was nothing metal on my license. I took the license out of my pocket, and they tried it again. It went off again. The fellow checking me said, "You must still have something in your pocket." I felt around and found a tiny piece of tin foil. It's amazing how that machine could find such a tiny piece of tin foil. It sort of reminds us that people may not be aware of our sins, but not even a little white lie can escape the sight of our heavenly Father. After being checked at the Detroit airport, we boarded the plane and flew into Orlando. We made hotel arrangements right away and began our nine fun-filled days at Disney.

The temperature was only forty degrees during our first few days in Florida. Sandy bought a Donald Duck jacket to help keep her warm, and I bought a Pluto hat. My hat was not so much to keep me warm as it was to help me look good. To tell you the truth, it would take more than a Pluto hat to make me look good. Maybe plastic surgery, but right now, that's not going to happen. I wore the Pluto hat all week.

We saw many things while at Disney including parades, light displays, scenes from some of the Disney movies, and much more. There were many rides, but because I don't particularly care for rides, I only went on a few. My favorite ride was Soarin. It was hardly a ride. You were in a chair that went up in the air. When you got to a certain height, you stopped, and they started showing scenes. It gave you the feeling you were flying. You'd fly over pine trees. You could fly over an orange grove and smell the oranges. You flew over the water, and without thinking, you lifted your feet so they wouldn't get wet. It was awesome! We experienced so many wonderful things at Disney.

What captivated me most happened on Friday night. Sandy and I were sitting on a bench waiting for Paul and Sierra to ride the stunt cars. Our plan was to ride Soarin again when they returned. While they were gone, a heart-wrenching thing happened. Kids could buy autograph books and collect autographs from the Disney characters as these dressed-up people walked around the park. While we were sitting on the bench, a young girl sat down next to us. We could easily tell she was mentally challenged. She laid her autograph book on the bench and took out her pen and brought them over to me. She saw my Pluto hat and thought I was one of the Disney characters. I was overwhelmed. Being her Pluto, I signed her book and said, "Honey, would you like to scratch my ear for me?"

She said, "Sure." As she scratched the ear on my Pluto hat, I got my leg going like a dog when he scratches fleas. Her mom and dad were laughing.

Her mom said, "Honey, look at his leg." She never did because she just kept looking into the face of her Pluto. She got Pluto's autograph that night. Besides that, she got someone to pray for her the rest of her life. She touched my heart that night, and it will never be the same.

One evening when my son Paul and his family were staying with us, I asked Paul if I could borrow his car to go see my friend Larry. Larry was a patient at the hospital and would be for some time. Paul said I could use his car, a pretty green one. I'm not a car buff, so I couldn't tell you the make or model. I just knew it was transportation. I drove to the hospital and parked the car. I went inside and asked a nurse what room Larry was in. She gave me his number, and I found Larry's room. Larry was glad to see me as I was him. We talked until I looked out the window and saw it was already dark. I told Larry how good it had been to talk with him, but I had to head for home. As I left the hospital, I was in for a big shock. I couldn't see Paul's pretty green car anywhere. I looked from one end of the parking lot to the other end, and it just was not there. How was I going to tell Paul someone had taken his car? As I started walking home, all I could think of was Paul left his car in my care, and now it was gone. I fretted all the way home, and by the time I got home, I was almost in tears. "Paul," I said, "while I was in the hospital, someone took your car." Paul told me to calm down. We would go back to the hospital and look some more. I said I had looked all over, and it wasn't there. Paul's wife Gina said she would call the police. Paul told her to wait until we got back from the hospital. I went to the hospital with Paul.

When we got to the hospital parking lot, Paul said, "That's my car over there." The parking lot lights shining on Paul's car through the darkness made his car appear blue. Boy did I feel stupid. It was sure good for a laugh at my expense. I think God uses things like this to keep us humble. This reminds me of an episode of the *Andy Griffith Show*.

The city council decided that it would get the school kids involved in helping to raise money for the orphanage. Each of the children were to try and raise money or bring a part of their allowance to their teacher, and the teacher would turn it over to the council when it was all turned in. Andy said to Barney, "Barn, I think this will do the kids a world of good giving to kids that have a lot less than they do. I can hardly wait to see how much Opie has given. I'll bet he gives more than all the other kids."

"I think you're right," Barney said. "He's always helping others." As Andy and Barney talked, they meandered over to the school. When they got there, they asked the teacher how the collection for the orphanage was coming. The teacher told them the collection was coming in pretty fast. A lot of the kids are bringing in quite a bit of money. Andy asked her how much Opie had given. She told him Opie hadn't given anything yet. As they left the school, Andy was furious. "I can't believe Opie hasn't given even one red cent," Andy fumed. They walked back to the sheriff's office. When Opie arrived from school, Andy was still upset. Andy spoke slowly trying not to say anything he might regret later. "Young man, your teacher tells me you haven't given any money for the orphans. Is that right."

"Yes, paw," Opie said. "I didn't have any money to give."

Andy's blood pressure rose again. "Opie, I want you to go home and think about how much you have and how little these orphans have. I will speak to you again when I get home."

When Andy arrived home, he spoke to Opie. "Son, have you thought about our earlier conversation?"

"Yes, paw," Opie said, "and you were right. I will give three cents."

Andy blurted out, "You go to your room and don't come down for supper."

Andy paced around the kitchen mumbling about how he was ashamed of how little Opie appreciated all he had.

Aunt Bea stopped Andy in his tracks. "Now, Andy, you know Opie is a good boy. He always does his chores, and he does really well in school. He always obeys us, and he never gets into trouble. Can't you let it go just this once?"

"You're right, Aunt Bea. I'll call Opie down for supper."

"Opie, would you come down here please?"

"What is it, paw?" Opie asked.

"I've been thinking, Opie, and if you don't want to give very much this time, it's okay."

"No, paw," Opie broke in. "It's not like that, you see there's this girl at school. Her name is Sally."

"Oh it's all right, Opie, if you want to take Sally to the movies. It's okay. You can even buy her some popcorn."

"No, paw, Sally's winter coat is wore out. I've been saving my money to buy her a new one."

"Opie, can't her mom buy her a new one?"

"No, paw, Sally's mom is poor and can barely keep food on the table. I figured if I saved, I could have enough money to buy her a coat by the time cold weather sets in."

"By the way, paw, I'm hungry. What's for supper?"

"Well, son, you and Aunt Bea are having fried chicken. I'm eating crow."

In September of 2007, I went to the doctor for my yearly checkup. I had blood work done in advance. My doctor started out by telling me my blood sugar was fine. He then told me my cholesterol was a little high, and since I had a stent, I should start working on lowering it. "Doctor, I don't have a stent," I said.

His response was, "You don't?"

I thought, *He has my records in his computer right in front of him. How could he not know I didn't have a stent?*

Sandy and I both felt it was time to find a new doctor. After some waiting, Dr. John Persson and his wife, Susan, took us as patients. Dr. Susan Persson checked me over and asked several questions. She asked me to come back in a week. When I returned, she said she had talked it over with her husband, and they both agreed that since my PSA was a little high in September, and since my dad died of prostate cancer at age seventy-two, they thought it would be a good idea if I would see an urologist. I saw Dr. Daniel Reum who did a biopsy. He took six pieces, and all came back cancerous. The prostate gland was removed; now, four years later, I am cancer free.

Thinking back, I am convinced that no doctor, having the patient's records in front of him, is ignorant enough to tell him he has a stent when he doesn't. The only thing I can see is God made him speak those words knowing if I didn't leave that doctor, I would never discover I had cancer. I'd still be walking around full of cancer thinking everything was okay when in reality I was death waiting to happen.

While I was still in the hospital following my prostate surgery, I ran into my old doctor. He said, "Bruce, they didn't tell me you were here in the hospital." I beat around the bush not wanting to tell him I found another doctor. I went back to my room and was sitting on the bed; there was a knock on the door, and it was my old doctor. He said, "Bruce, they didn't tell me you left us."

Then I told him, "Doctor, I think God ordained it. If I hadn't left you, I would have never found out I had cancer." I told him everything in a nice way, and he left I am still alive and better because I left him. I pray he learns from his mistake and is a better doctor because of it.

Sandy and I love having our granddaughters visit us. One time when Sierra was nearly one year old and Megan was just under two, they told me they would like a gummy bear Popsicle. We didn't have any in our freezer, so I told the girls we would go to the store and buy some gummy bears. We went to Meijer, and they didn't have any. We went to Shop-and-Save to discover they had none. Sierra had fallen asleep by this time. She was getting heavy to carry, so I told Megan we would take Sierra back home where she would be more comfortable, and we would hunt more. Sierra was so tired that when we took her home and laid her on our bed, she never woke up.

Megan and I continued our popsicle search by going to Wal-Mart. Before we left the car, I told Megan we would pray about it. We went into the store to discover they didn't have any either. What they did have was "sunken treasure" popsicles. They were a pretty blue. Inside these were gummy sharks, gummy dolphins, and gummy treasure chest. I had never seen these before nor since. That's why I know God put them there just for us. Isn't God good!

Another time when the girls were with us, I asked Megan to go to the store with me. We completed our errand and walked toward our car. As I started to get into the car, Megan said, "No, Grandpa, that's not our car." Sure enough it was a car that looked just like ours and was parked next to ours. I thought that was amazing—a two-year-old granddaughter saw the difference and I didn't.

It started out like any other Sunday morning. I got up and spent time with the Lord. I sang a couple songs God had given me. I praised God for how great he is and how I never wanted to live without him. I told him all the prayer needs from my prayer list. I read one day from *Our Daily Bread* and read some scripture.

Sandy got up, and I put her tea water on while she checked her blood on her diabetes meter. We sat for a while and watched Fox News. We then started getting around for church. Sandy started getting dressed while I got my shower. She had her shower the night before. When we were finished getting dressed, we went to church. We love going to church and worshipping and loving God; we couldn't get along without him. We also love the people we worship with. After church we went out to eat.

When we got home, we changed into clothes that were more comfortable. I took my pants and underwear down and was surprised to see blood in the front of my underwear. I hadn't noticed it before, but there was also blood on the towel I had dried on that morning. Every time I went to the bathroom, I checked to see if there was blood in my urine, but there never was. The next day, I made an appointment with the urologist. When we saw him, he asked if I had any blood in the urine. I told him I kept checking and never saw any. I told him I had been having a lot of back pain. He told me back pain had nothing to do with the problem I was having. He said he would send me for a CAT scan and he would also run a camera up my penis and then maybe we could get to the bottom of what was going on. I had my CAT scan and was back to Dr. Reum's office for the camera treatment.

While I was still under anesthetic, Dr. Reum showed Sandy the pictures he had taken. He kept saying he couldn't believe what big honkers they were. He was referring to two of the cysts on my kidneys. The largest was the size of a softball or a little bigger. He told Sandy maybe that is the cause of my back pain. When I came around, he told me that I had cysts on my kidneys, and he was going to send me to the hospital to have the largest one drained.

A couple of days later, I went to the hospital to have the cyst drained. The nurse prepared me for the removal of the liquid from the cyst. The doctor came in and gave me a shot to deaden the pain. That surely worked. I never felt another thing. As they were draining the cyst, I was talking to the doctor. I asked him if the liquid in the cyst was blood. He told me to wait a minute, and he would show me as the first flask was almost full. I told him it looked like a glass of beer. He said, "Yeah, and there's even a head on it."

I said, "Is it urine?"

He said, "That's exactly what it is." After I had it drained, my back felt much better.

Dr. Reum told me he would set up an appointment with a kidney specialist in Muskegon. What would he say to me? Better yet what would he do to me? Then a different idea came into my head. A woman in our church just had cysts on her kidneys, and they sent her to Ann Arbor and had them removed. That made me simmer down. If a lady who was older than me could do it, so could I.

When I met the kidney doctor, he had a surprise for me. He told me I could not have the cysts removed. I didn't just have cysts! I had kidney disease. He told me I probably had it all my life. My first thought was if I had kidney disease all my life, God was really taking care of me since I am now seventy-four years old. He said a lot of things that my mind was trying to understand. One thing he told me was something about with this disease, it could go to the brain. I answered by saying that it sounded like and aneurysm. He said that was exactly what it was. He said there were two options. The first option was surgery. That wasn't a very good option. If I had surgery, I would be on dialysis the rest of my life. The second one was to wait until the cysts grew to a size that was causing me pain and drain it like we did the last one. We both thought that was the best option.

A week later, I had another appointment with Dr. Reum. I told him that the kidney doctor told me I had kidney disease. He said, "I told you, you had kidney disease. I told you blah, blah, blah, blah blah." The blahs are in place of the medical words. I guess because he had a medical degree, I should understand his doctor language. I guess because I don't makes me stupid. Maybe because I know Jesus and he doesn't, maybe that makes him more stupid than I am. I guess that is like dumb and dumber.

I've had tests and been seen by my VA doctor and the kidney doctor twice since then. My VA doctor told me I didn't have to worry about the kidney disease. He said my kidneys are functioning better than the kidneys of most people my age.

When I went back to the kidney doctor and told him what the VA doctor said, he agreed with him. He said the tests he saw said the same thing. He said I would not have to come back to him for a year. He then told me if I got a headache worse than any I had ever had, I should go to the hospital. He said I would probably have an aneurysm.

The fact that I've had kidney disease for seventy-four years and my kidneys are functioning better than I have any right to expect that tells me that all through the years my God has been holding me in the palm of his hands. Isn't our loving God good?

October 30, I woke up to meet another day. I enjoy the early morning hours because it is quiet, and I can grab a cup of coffee and sit down and have my quiet time with the Lord before starting the day's activities. Today was different however; today I was fasting. Dr. Persson always orders blood work that has to have fasting. I hate fasting; it disrupts the whole morning. No cup of decaf coffee, no breakfast, no getting the morning off on the right foot. What a bummer.

The time came to go to the hospital for my blood testing. I was in second gear. I got to the hospital and didn't have to wait very long:

The young lady took two vials of blood and gave me a plastic cup for a urine sample. Wow the time at the hospital wasn't as long as I thought. I got home and had my coffee and breakfast, awesome. It's going to be a great day after all. No more fasting for another six months, so I thought.

November 5, I woke up, took a deep breath, and got out of bed. It was going to be a good day. I had my morning decaf coffee, sat down at the table, and had my morning talk with the Lord. What a great morning. I skipped the morning breakfast and got to save a couple of pounds when I step on the scales at the doctor's office. I guess I had better get a shower so that I'll look and smell good at the doctor's office. At 9:45, I guess I had better leave for my appointment which is at 10:15. I sure don't want to be late. At 10:15, the nurse called me in and had me step on the scale. That breakfast I didn't eat should help the weight. She took me into a room and checked my blood pressure, pulse, and temperature. She told me the doctor would be in shortly. They always say that even if it is an hour. He was in, however, in a few minutes. He didn't give me very good news. He said I gained six pounds, my blood pressure was high, my blood sugar was high, and my salt level was high. He said he was going to send me for more blood work the next day.

November 6, I woke to another day of fasting. By this time, you know how I love fasting—not. On a scale of 1–10, 1 being the least and 10 being the most love for fasting, my love for fasting is 0. I had to busy myself until seven o'clock 'til I could go and get my blood work done. It wasn't so bad. In fact, it was the highlight of the day. I spent most of that time in fellowship with the Lord. He could have told me how this was my own fault for overeating, but he didn't. He just let me talk and get my frustration out of my system. I felt much better. It's funny how the Lord knows just what to do, and yet he knows how to take care of us. He created us.

At seven o'clock, I went and got my blood work done. The rest of the morning was rather uneventful. At noon, I grabbed a bite to eat. Who am I trying to kid? It was quite a bit more than a bite. At one o'clock, I got a call from Dr. Persson's office. Rick told me because I had diabetes, Dr. John told him to set me up with diet classes. I told Rick that Dr. Persson didn't tell me I had diabetes. Rick said the doctor should have told me, but he told him too, so he was just following orders. He told me I had classes on November 13, 22, and December 2, 3, and 4. I told Rick, "You know, Rick, my wife only had two classes, and my son Paul only had one class." That must make me really stupid if I have to have five classes.

Rick kind of laughed and said, "No, Bruce, it's just the way they do things now."

After I hung up from talking to Rick, I did a lot of soul search-ing. Maybe God allowed me to have diabetes so I would take my weight seriously. God only gives us good gifts, but he can allow us to have a bad one if it's for our own good. I thought if gaining six pounds caused me to get diabetes, and so if I lost some pounds, I might be able to get rid of diabetes. I made up my mind. I needed to make changes in my eating habits. I decided since my salt level was high, I would stop putting salt on my food. If I felt I needed seasoning. I would put pepper on my food. I also decided to try and eat less during the day. I also would look at what I drank. My coffee was okay. I already changed to decaf coffee and had stopped putting sugar in it. I love Hawaiian punch. I knew there had to be a lot of sugar in it, so I stopped drinking it and started drinking nothing but decaf coffee and water. In the first week, I lost ten pounds. I was proud of myself.

I had to go back to see Dr. John on the twelfth of November. I could hardly wait. This was the first time I was really excited about going to the doctor because of my weight. I knew he would be pleased with me too. When I went however, I was disappointed. Rick, an assistant, checked me this time. Rick was happy for me. He couldn't believe I lost ten pounds in a week. When he checked all my vitals, they were getting back to near normal. He gave me a machine and test strips to check my blood sugar and told me the doctor wanted me to check them twice a day. When I left, I told Rick to be sure to show my weight to Dr. John. He said he was happy to do it.

November 13, I went to my first class. I didn't want to be here. I had already made up my mind how I would lose weight and better my health, but because Dr. John wanted me to take these classes, I decided I would come and make the most of it.

Kristen, the instructor for the first day, said she was glad to see I was already working on my weight. The second day, I would have Rebecca. They were two fine ladies and instructors. They shared the next three meetings. There were four of us in the last three classes, three guys and one girl. I was the only one that wasn't on diabetes insulin. I was in the one hundred range. I don't know about the girl, but one of the guys was in the two hundred range, and the other one was in the three hundred range. In my first meeting with Kristin, she asked me what the worse thing was about finding out that I had diabetes. I said finding out that I had to attend these meetings. We laughed about that. I really found out it wasn't so bad. We learned a lot about the food we eat, the good ones and the bad ones. We also learned how important exercise is. I guess I already knew about exercise, but I tried to ignore it as much as I could.

I really felt sorry for the two guys in the class. Where they were at with their blood sugar, they could have a heart attack or a stroke at any minute. I don't know where the girl was at, but from how she talked in class, it was like, she was doing the things she should.

I have lost ten more pounds so far, but now I seem, to be at a standstill. My biggest problem is I haven't been faithful with my exercise. I need to get back on course with it. I promised myself I would be down to two hundred pounds by the time I go back to see Dr. John. That's ten more pounds and two and a half months away. I can make it but not without exercise. I will make it.

My son Paul and my sister-in-law Connie both had bariatric surgery. I don't know about Connie, but Paul had tried different weight loss systems without any success. I haven't talked to Connie, but I think her and Paul both felt this was the best way to get their health back on track.

So far after three weeks, Paul has lost twenty-six pounds, and Connie, I haven't talked to her recently, but after two weeks, she had lost twenty-four pounds. They both have done what they had to do to get their health back, and I am proud of them, and they should be too.

A few weeks ago, in Bible study, we were looking at John the second chapter. It was about Jesus turning the water into wine. It reads like this. On the third day, a wedding took place at Cana in Galilee. Jesus's mother was there, and Jesus and his disciples had also been invited to the wedding. When the wine was gone, Jesus's mother said to him, "They have no more wine."

"Dear woman, why do you involve me?" Jesus replied. "My time has not yet come." It goes on from there, and Jesus did turn the water into wine. As I thought about this, I wondered why Jesus turned the water into wine. Was it so the young married couple wouldn't be embarrassed or was it to honor his mother? As I thought about this, the Holy Spirit said to me, "Are you honoring your father and mother?"

I told the Holy Spirit I always honor my mother and try to honor my father the best I can. The Holy Spirit said, "Have you really? Do you think what you have written in this story has been fair to your dad?" I thought I had. "Do you think I haven't? From here on, I'm going to make it, Holy Spirit," I said. "Like a trial."

HOLY SPIRIT: Let's go back and see what you have written. On the bottom of page 8, you said, "He was not much of a husband or a father." A few sentences back, you said, "What I can tell you about them is very little and mostly what other people have told me." Is this correct?

BRUCE: I guess that's about it.

HOLY SPIRIT: You say your dad just gave your mom $5 toward caring for the family. Is that what someone else told you?

BRUCE: Yes, that's right.

HOLY SPIRIT: Didn't that person tell you they really loved your mom?

BRUCE: Yes.

HOLY SPIRIT: And didn't that person's son tell you his mother and your brother Duane got in a heated discussion because she said some bad things about your dad?

BRUCE: Yes.

HOLY SPIRIT: So doesn't it sound like that person loved your mom and couldn't or didn't have good things to say about your dad?

BRUCE: It does sound that way.

HOLY SPIRIT: So don't you think you should give your dad the benefit of the doubt?

BRUCE: Yes, I think you're right. But what about what he did taking a neighborhood kid to the show with him instead of me?

HOLY SPIRIT: Let's look at it. If you had gone home after school and did the dishes and then went back and played football, that would have never happened, would it?

BRUCE: No, but—

HOLY SPIRIT: Hold on. The fact that he went to the movies without you isn't the issue, is it?

BRUCE: No. I had that coming. It was the fact he took one of the neighborhood kids with him.

HOLY SPIRIT: The fact that he took one of the neighborhood kids with him, Bruce, does not mean you don't mean any more than you do. It hadn't been long after your mom died. You know how bad you were feeling. As bad as you were feeling, he was probably feeling worse. He had just lost his wife and best friend and probably just didn't want to be alone. Can you understand, Bruce?

BRUCE: As much as I don't want to I guess I do understand. But—

HOLY SPIRIT: But you still aren't really sure he loved you. Right?

BRUCE: Yes.

HOLY SPIRIT: Do you remember when you were little? One Christmas your dad made you a gun set? He was a shoemaker at the time. He made the holster set out of a material like buckskin and the guns out of something like hard rubber. I think you really liked that set, didn't you?

BRUCE: I loved that set. I was so proud of it.

HOLY SPIRIT: Would you say that was a labor of love?

BRUCE: It had to have been. It had to have taken hours.

HOLY SPIRIT: Do you think he would have done it for one of the neighborhood kids?

BRUCE: No. I don't think so.

HOLY SPIRIT: Do you remember you said your mother sent you to Sunday school every Sunday except the Sundays you could get your dad to take you fishing with him?

BRUCE: Yes. I remember it sure was fun.

HOLY SPIRIT: Do you also remember your dad taking heat from your mom for taking you?

BRUCE: Yes, Mom really got upset with him.

HOLY SPIRIT: Do you think he would risk the anger of his wife and best friend if he didn't love you?

BRUCE: You're right, Holy Spirit, he did love me. Tell my father I am sorry, and I don't know if it matters now, but tell my dad I'm sorry and I love him too.

Several years ago, I decided I would like to have an Easter egg hunt for our grandchildren. Sandy agreed to this also. We gave them candy, presents, and mostly money. We put nickels, dimes, and quarter and some dollars in their eggs. This became a big family tradition. The first year, the older kids seemed to get more than the younger; this was true. The first year was experimental, leaving room for improvement. This event was as though they were getting two Christmases. Maybe all of this was because we loved our grandchildren so much or perhaps it was because I figured by giving them two Christmases, it would make up for some of the Christmases I was cheated out of. Maybe it was a little of both. My granddaughter Tess wrote the following story about the Ester egg hunt. I want you to read it.

The Colossal Easter Egg Hunt

It was a very warm Friday, and it was getting very close to Easter. "When are we going to Grandma and Grandpa's house?" I asked.

Mother replied, "Today, after school." We were driving for a while, and my two brothers and I just would not be quiet. We were excited to be going to our grandparents' house. We sometimes would get the dog hyped, so he would bark. An hour and a half later, we arrived in Ludington. My parents put most of our stuff in the house, and we helped a little. The kids went to the small television. We watched television while the adults were cooking. We had lasagna for dinner. It was pretty good. After that, I practiced playing the piano. I learned how to play "Lightly Row" and "When the Saints Go Marching In." Then I got into the stuff in the blue shed in the backyard. I got out a blue-green bike and a really old "Green Machine." I fell in love with the bike because it was too big for me, but I rode it anyway.

The next day, we woke up to the clanking of pans and the scent of pancakes. My grandpa makes awesome pancakes—even better than my mom and dad. When breakfast was over, I asked grandpa, "When do we search for our Easter baskets?"

He told me, "We don't do that anymore. We will be doing an Easter egg hunt, and Grandma Bunny and Grandpa Bunny will be handing out presents too." But first, we had to paint their faces for the occasion. The day was progressing nicely, and the sun was coming out, making it nice and toasty. After a while, we painted Grandma's face pink with great big buck teeth and Grandpa's face green with mammoth buck teeth; they looked hysterical. While we were painting faces, the adults were hiding money-filled eggs. When they said it was okay to look, we started the colossal Easter egg hunt. When we were stumped, they would give us clues, "You're getting colder or hotter."

We finished a backbreaking thirty minutes later. Okay, it wasn't that long, but it seemed that way. We then cracked open the eggs and put our treasures in plastic bags. I got my first fake fur kitty like Grandma and my cousins had. I also got a DVD of *Harry Potter and the Goblet of Fire*, not to mention candy. My grandpa enjoys making a big deal out of Easter because he thinks Easter is a very important holiday, and he enjoys watching the kids have fun with it. Would you think that this is a colossal Easter or what? We do!

The end.

8
CHAPTER

W here did they all go? It's 12:40 a.m. on July 20, 2015, Monday morning. I took an early afternoon snooze, and now I can't sleep. Sandy said I wouldn't be able to sleep, but I thought I was tired enough to sleep. As usual, Sandy was right.

When I said, "Where did they all go?" I was referring to all those years attending the Free Methodist Church in Ludington. There is no Free Methodist Church anymore. There was only eleven of us left, so we had no choice but to close the doors. How did we get down to this? I guess I will have to start at the beginning.

It was 1976, and we had just left the United Methodist Church. Sandy's brother Hal and his wife, Karen, asked us if we would try their church as long as we had left the other church. We said that we would. Our son Paul wasn't happy. He hadn't wanted to leave the United Methodist Church. He said he had just gotten out of the baby class, and he didn't want to leave.

We went to the Free Methodist Church that first Sunday. Sandy and I liked it, but the boys would also have to like it in order for us to return. On the way home, we asked the boys how they liked it. They both said they liked it and asked us if we could return next Sunday.

Sunday evenings there was an evening service called the hour of inspiration. People would share Bible verses that meant a lot to help them, and they would tell how God's son Jesus had helped them through difficult times. It was always an awesome hour. I already told you how Jesus saved me in one of these services.

It seems like there just wasn't enough time to spend with the Lord. We finally started small groups after Sunday evening services.

I held one in our house, and we had several people from our church come, plus Sandy's mom and dad came, and sometimes they brought other couples also.

David Johnston was our pastor. He was a young pastor, and I think he was growing right along with his congregation. He and his wife, Ann, had been in Ludington for two years, and they would serve one more year.

The conference had asked Pastor Dave to do something he felt he could not comply with, so at the end of 1977, David and Ann left the Free Methodist Church.

I always thought it kind of strange we had come from the Methodist Church and came to the Free Methodist Church. David and Ann left the Free Methodist Church and went to a Methodist Church.

This wasn't the last time we had contact with Pastor David and Ann. Like I said before, we took a summer vacation with Lynn Thomson and his family. I mentioned that on the way to Cedar Point, we stopped at his brother's house. I didn't mention that we also stopped at Pastor David and Anna's house. We went to church with them, had dinner with them, and then in the afternoon we made ice cream. We had a swell time. We then went on to Cedar Point.

We had no more contact with them until a few years ago. Sandy and I were attempting to collect pictures of all the pastors and their wives that we worshiped with. I called and talked to Pastor David, and he said he would be glad to send us one.

When it was very certain we would be a Free Methodist Church no more, Sandy and I decided to start sending the pictures back to the pastors. I called and let him know why we were sending them back and to be expecting them.

When I called the Johnston phone number, Ann answered. We talked for a while, and she told me David was now retired. He hadn't had any hobbies, Ann said, so he took training and became a tour bus driver. She said he really loves it.

When Pastor David and Ann left, they had just started a new year, and the conference did not have any Free Methodist pastor to send us. They did find a retired Wesleyan pastor and his wife to send us. So we started two years under the leadership of Pastor Vernon and Harriett Draggoo. They were two of the most Godly and loving people I have ever had the honor to know. When their two years were up, they would have liked to stay, but the conference had found us a Free Methodist pastor, so they were not invited back.

Pastor Carlton and Jean Rauch became our new pastor couple. I don't know much about their background except Pastor Rauch had been in the navy. Although I received my lay minister's license under Pastor Draggoo, I grew the most in my Christian faith under Pastor Rauch. He was a great encouragement to me. Sometimes he would just give me a pat on the back. Other times, he would give me a compliment. He would say the book report I handed him was so good, he could write a sermon from it.

The greatest thing I can say about Pastor Rauch is the fact he lived his faith in Jesus. When he went fishing, he didn't catch as many fish as he could have. He spent more time going up and down the riverbank fishing for men. It was more important to him to tell people about Jesus rather than catching fish. Outside of Jesus, he's still my hero.

The next pastor and his wife that came was Bob and Debbie Brail. They had been school teachers in Iowa. I don't know why they decided to go into the ministry. I can only think that because his dad was a pastor, there was a strong pull from family. He did a good job as a pastor, but I don't really believe his heart was in it. He eventually left and went back into teaching.

While he was here, he told us he had always wanted a trophy. Since he had never won one, he bought one at a yard sale. While he was here, Sandy and I bowled with Pastor Bob and Debbie and won first place trophies. He was so glad he could finally say that he won a trophy.

He also played on our softball team. When they left, I went from first to third base and brought my son Paul in from the outfield to play first base. Bringing Paul in to play first base was one of the best decisions I ever made as a manager. Paul became one of the best first basemen in our league, if not the best. One tournament we were in, Paul got the defensive player of the tournament award.

The last I talked to Pastor Bob, they were living in Defiance, Missouri. I still miss them.

Our next pastor was Pastor David Burton. He was not only a pastor; he also did concrete work. His wife, Bessie, once said to him, "How much money do you need in a week?" I don't want you to think that from that one line that she was a crab or a grumpy person. She was one of the sweetest people you could ever meet. I also don't want you to think from that, that Pastor Dave was money hungry. The fact is that ever since he was young, he loved working with concrete.

Pastor Dave also did a lot of calling on people in the neighborhood. Sandy's aunt and uncle lived about two or three blocks from the church. Sandy's dad always told her that you would never see them in church. Pastor Dave called on them quite often. He not only talked with them, but he also shoveled snow and other things for them. Sandy was surprised one day to see them walk into the church. They became regular attendees. Isn't it wonderful what God can do when his people show his love?

Pastor Dave has been doing a lot of work at our church camp at Manton. He also did some typing for me. I still talk to him on the phone once in a while.

Pastor Mark Bullock and his wife, Cindy, were the next couple to become the Free Methodist pastorate in Ludington. Mark's dad had been a pastor also, and Mark grew up in his pastorate in Boyne City, Michigan. Pastor Mark was a good pastor, and his wife, Cindy, led music. Pastor Mark helped to grow the church. Under the leadership of Pastor Mark, the church was averaging in the mid-eighties.

Although things seemed to be going well, Cindy was not happy. She was told that she would never be able to have a baby. A lot of prayers went out for Cindy. Some time passed, and Pastor Mark and Cindy found a girl who was pregnant and didn't want to keep her baby. Pastor Mark and Cindy made arrangements to take her baby. There was now happiness in the Bullock household. They now had a bouncing baby boy by the name of Cody. I don't think there was one person in the Ludington Free Methodist Church that didn't love Pastor Mark and Cindy, but that didn't stop them from leaving. Pastor Mark heard that the church in Boyne City was near closing. Pastor Mark and Cindy did a lot of soul searching and praying. Pastor Mark was raised in the Boyne City church. He felt maybe he could keep the Boyne City church from closing. Pastor Mark decided to go even though he really wanted to stay in Ludington.

Even though Pastor Mark gave it his best, the Boyne City church still closed its doors for the last time. The conference moved Pastor Mark to Evart. They are still there and doing well.

When they left, some of the people left also, so when Pastor Bill and Darlene Moede came, they didn't get a fair shake. The conference didn't help them much, even though they should have. It didn't help matters that one woman in the church called the district superintendent and told him people were leaving the church because of them. I called the district superintendent and told him that what she had told him was not true, that people had left the church before he even preached his first sermon. The district superintendent called Pastor Bill and told him that he shouldn't have got me involved in this matter. It's kind of strange how one person can make their views known to the conference but another one can't. It made me feel like a second class citizen.

Pastor Bill and Darlene were only here a short time; I feel it was a good couple of years. I feel Pastor Bill grew as a pastor in his time at Ludington even though he got very little help from the conference. Pastor Bill and Darlene also spent a lot of time visiting homes and nursing homes. They wanted to make sure the elderly weren't forgotten.

They are now pastoring down south in Alabama and Tennessee. They still get a little flack, but all and all, the people on a whole love and respect them. Sandy and I still keep in contact with them. We wanted them to know that someone in Ludington still loves them.

I don't want you to think that no one else in Ludington cared about them because there is still a few people in Ludington who do.

Our next pastor was Kyle Segar. He had been a successful businessman, but he felt God's calling for him to be a pastor. He filled in a few times in our church, and then the conference made him our full-time pastor.

It was hard for quite a while. We did a lot of praying, and God was still working on our behalf. Things started happening. The Washington Avenue Baptist Church was building a new church, and so they were selling their old church. It was a lot newer and a lot bigger than our church. Although we were a small congregation, we did a lot of praying again. God heard our prayers. Because we were a small congregation, it was a large step of faith when we bought the Baptist Church. It was a debt we never got out from under.

For a while, good things started happening. We got our old church sold. That helped our money problems for a while. Then a young couple named Sarah and Kelly came to our church. They had just moved into town and had attended a Free Methodist Church, so it was only natural that they would look for another church in the same denomination. After they came, a police officer and his family came. They liked it, and so he invited two other officers and their families to come. Soon our church was doing good. We were making enough to pay the bills. We hadn't been doing this good since Pastor Mark left.

Our church never got going again. We were doing very well for some time, but then Sarah and Kelly made a move so that they could be closer to their family. After this, the police officers and their families also left. After some time, our pastor, who had taken two pay cuts, also left when he found another church.

Our church never recovered. Either the conference couldn't find another pastor for our church or we just weren't large enough to salvage. It was a sad day, but we had to close our doors for the last time.

I always felt that God wanted me to stay in the Free Methodist Church. I felt God had big plans for the church, and He wanted me to be part of it. I guess I was wrong.

We aren't smart enough to know what God is thinking. The smartest thing we can do is wait for God's lead. The first thing we had to do was find a church. We knew we would never make God happy if we went to a cult, so that ruled them out. We felt the Catholic Church was also not happening. There were lots of reasons they are out, but I will only tell you one. I don't have to confess my thoughts to a priest. When Jesus died on the cross, the curtain was torn in half between the Holy of Holies and the rest of the church. That was a sign that since Jesus died for our sins; we could take our problem and our sins directly to God. We couldn't choose a Lutheran church for they are just a breakoff of the Catholic Church. We really didn't think we would feel comfortable in a Baptist Church because they believe once saved, always saved. They believe that way because Jesus said, "I will never lose those you have given me Father." This is true, but God has made us people with a free will. Jesus won't lose those God gave Him, but having a free choice, we can walk away.

The first Sunday we decided to attend the Wesleyan Church of Scottville. It was about a five-mile drive. After the first Sunday, we knew this was where we were going to stay. It was like coming home.

Roger Warmuskerken was the pastor along with his wife, Marilyn. They loved the congregation, and it shows. The congregation returns their love, and it makes for a church that is full of love. I have not heard one bad word about anyone. That's how it should be, one happy family.

When we were there a short time, someone told pastor that we sang songs that God had given me. He asked us if we would like to do special music some Sunday. We said we would. Since then, we have been doing special music about once a month. We sing without musical support, so I hope people don't get tired of us.

9
CHAPTER

Last month, I went to the funeral home to pay my respect to Val Taylor Jr. who had lost his battle with cancer. We greeted Val's wife and soul mate, Pat. It was going to be hard for Pat to get used to not having Val with her. They were always together. As I think back to my teen years, Val and I were always together. He was my best friend. We both loved to bowl. We both bowled several times a week. Val was an excellent bowler. I could never beat him. If I had a great game, he had one just a little better.

We also both loved baseball. One Friday night, on the spur of the moment, we decided to go to Detroit and watch the Tigers play. We hadn't ever gone to a big league game before, so this was a big venture. Val borrowed his brother Don's car, and we headed to Detroit. We drove all night and got to Detroit in the early morning. It was sprinkling but not very hard. We were sure they would still play. When it was game time, we went into the stadium and looked around after we had bought our tickets. It was awesome. It is hard to imagine two teen boys taking on such a huge task, but here we were standing in the confines of Tigers stadium.

This was the home of all those great Tigers players we routed for. I say it again, it was awesome. We found a vendor and bought a hot dog, and we looked around some more. All of a sudden, we stopped in our tracks. The worse thing that could possibly happen, happened. The game was called because of rain. How could they call it? It wasn't raining; it was sprinkling. Whatever you call it, they still called the game. What a bummer. We headed for home. When we got to Lansing, we found a bowling alley. We bowled several games, so the trip wasn't a total loss.

I was brought back to the present when I heard my name called. I was pleased to see Val's sister Beverly and her husband, Buzz. I hadn't seen them since I was a teenager. They asked how I was doing, and I told them I was doing fine. Buzz said, "When you were young, you were so skinny you could hardly hold a bowling ball. Now look at you."

I said, "Thanks, Buzz, I don't know if I should take that as a compliment or a slam." We all had a good laugh.

My mind started wandering back once again to those teen years. I knew I would never go to college, so I took as many easy classes as I could. The only hard class I took was French. Ms. Cooper was my French teacher. I worked hard trying to get an A. I studied and turned in extra credit work. I asked Ms. Cooper if I was in line to get an A grade. She said no, my pronunciation was terrible. I was very upset; I wanted revenge. I knew I couldn't torment her in class any more than I already was. I decided I had to go by the old saying, "The pen is mightier than the sword." I decided to write a story and make her the villain. The trouble was she liked it better than anyone.

Cast

Bruce: student and hero of the story

Mr. Hartman: principal and victim of the theft

Mr. Crislieb: Latin teacher. His favorite saying when students were getting out of control was "People."

Mr. Mathis: Drama teacher, nice guy. He and the janitor are victimized by the writer.

Ms. Cooper: French teacher and villain of the story

Dragged Net of the School

This is the school house, Ludington high school. I am a student. I slave here.

(Dum, de, dum, dum, dum, dum, de, dum, dum, dum.)

9:15: Monday morning, I was called out of class and asked to report to the principal's office.

9:18: I arrived at the principal's office and reluctantly entered. As I entered, Mr. Hartman took off his glasses and began wiping the tears from his eyes. I never thought he would be this happy to see me.

Bruce: Now, now, Mr. Hartman, I'm glad to see you too, but you don't have to cry about it

Mr. Hartman: I'm not crying because I'm glad to see you, you idiot. I'm crying because some crude, obnoxious, oblivious, thickheaded, numbskull has taken revenge on me.

Bruce: You...you mean someone came in here and beat you?

Mr. Hartman: Ah, that it were so, it would be a far, far better fate.

Bruce: Mr. Hartman, quit hamming it up and tell me what happened.

Mr. Hartman: Over the weekend, someone broke into the school.

Bruce: Did they steal anything valuable?

Mr. Hartman: Did they steal anything valuable? Did they steal anything valuable? I'll say they did, and unless someone can crack this case, it'll just about ruin me.

Bruce: For the last time, Mr. Hartman, what did they steal?

Mr. Hartman: My Marilyn Monroe calendar.

Bruce: Nothing could be this serious. There was only one solution, bring the culprit to justice. Mr. Hartman, are there any clues?

Mr. Hartman: None.

Bruce: Mr. Hartman, keep this kind of confidential, but I think this is an inside job.

MR. HARTMAN: No.

BRUCE: Yes, I have been noticing how the other male teachers have been eyeing you with envy. Yes, even some of the more mature male students have been drooling too. There is no doubt in my mind that this is an inside job.

MR. HARTMAN: Those sly, old codgers, I didn't' think they had it in them.

Bruce: Mr. Hartman, do you want me to take this case? I once worked at Scotland Yard, you know!

MR. HARTMAN: While you were working at Scotland Yard, did you meet Sherlock Holmes?

BRUCE: No, the only Holmes I met while working at Scotland Lumberyard was a Ralph Holmes.

MR. HARTMAN: They're probably cousins.

BRUCE: By the way, Mr. Hartman, if I crack this case, what's in it for me?

MR. HARTMAN: If you crack this case, I'll see you get an A in French.

BRUCE: How are you going to get Ms. Copper to give me an A in French?

MR. HARTMAN: I'll give her a ten inches by twelve inches autographed picture of Tab Hunter.

BRUCE: Okay, but as a bonus, I want that picture you have of Jane Russell.

MR. HARTMAN: Anything, only get my calendar back.

As I began to leave the office, Mr. Hartman started babbling incoherently. I knew for Mr. Hartman's sake, I had better find the thief fast.

10:05: I ventured into the hallway to begin the case that I called "Who stole the Marilyn Monroe calendar?" or "The lost figure."

Not having any ideas where to start looking for clues, I decided to play Charlie Chan. Honorable ancestor say, when feeling mighty low, start in basemen. I decided to do the same.

As I approached the boiler room, I heard voices. I crept close to the door so I could hear the voices more clearly.

FIRST VOICE: Have you ever seen such hands before? Aren't they simply scrumptious?
SECOND VOICE: You're not just whistling Dixie.
FIRST VOICE: After all these years, I've finally done it.

I knew now that when I opened the door, I would have the thief in my grasp. I opened the door and rushed inside.

BRUCE: All right, I've finally caught you, you culprit.

I was rather surprised to see Mr. Mathis and the janitor.

MR. MATHIS: What are you talking about, you idiot?
BRUCE: Don't act innocent with me. I heard you talking about Mr. Hartman's Marilyn Monroe calendar.
MR. MATHIS: You must be crazy. We were just having a friendly game of poker.
BRUCE: Sure! Sure! You were just having a friendly game of poker, and I am Rock Hudson. Don't get cute with me. I heard you talking

about her hands, and how after all these
years you finally did it.

Mr. Mathis: I was talking about the poker hands
I've been getting.

Bruce: And...and what about what you said
about after all these years?

Mr. Mathis: That's right, after all these years, I
finally got a royal flush.

Oh well, anyone can be wrong once, and
since I was already here, I decided to join them
for a little poker.

10:35: I decided I better continue my
search. Not only that, a friendly game of poker
can get rather expensive.

Deep in thought, I found myself on the stairs
that led to the main floor. This case was quite
puzzling. There were still no clues. I reached the
main floor and kept walking. I passed room 12.
If only I had one little scrap of evidence to go on.
I came to room 10 and stopped short. I hurried
back to room 12. Something drastic must have
happened. I hadn't heard Mr. Crislieb's famous
cry of people. I then heard Mr. Crislieb's voice.

Mr. Crislieb: Oh, you precious idol you. You
are the most. Alone, we are nothing, but
together, we could conquer the world.

Oh well, everyone has to go sometime, but
I never thought of Mr. Crislieb as the lover boy
type. Just think, "Hot Lips" Crislieb.

I was about to open the door and rush
inside. But wait, what if I was wrong again! I
knew it was impossible, but if I was wrong again
and busted in on Mr. Crislieb's love scene, there

would be hell to pay. I decided the only thing to do was to become a Peeping Tom and look through the keyhole. What I saw made my eyes pop. Mr. Crislieb was talking to a statue of Julius Caesar.

11:10: I left from room 12 and headed for my locker. My stomach told me it was time to go to lunch. When I arrived at my locker, Mr. Hartman cornered me.

MR. HARTMAN: How come you're sneaking out early, and what have you found out about my calendar?

BRUCE: In the first place, a good detective always thinks better on a full stomach. In the second place, I haven't found out anything about your calendar. But what I've found out about some of the teachers in this school makes confidential look like kid's stuff. Even though Mr. Hartman offered me two pictures of bubble dancers, I would not reveal my secret. That is, not until he came across with two more pictures. I then left for lunch.

1:15: I returned to school to continue my search. I went to the principal's office. I had to see if Mr. Hartman had heard anything.

1:20: I arrived at the office. Mr. Hartman was pacing back and forth like an expectant father. I'll bet he hasn't done that in quite a while. As I entered, Mr. Hartman gave a big sigh of relief.

BRUCE: You look worried, Mr. Hartman.

MR. HARTMAN: I am worried, you clown. I can give you a white slip for one day, but after that, who knows what fortunes drift along the endless tides.

BRUCE: Well, Mr. Hartman, I didn't know you could quote Shakespeare.

MR. HARTMAN: That's not Shakespeare, you dope. I read that in a comic book.

BRUCE: By the way, Mr. Hartman, have you found any clues?

MR. HARTMAN: Yes and no.

BRUCE: Mr. Hartman, quit playing games. Have you found any clues or not?

MR. HARTMAN: Yes, I have a clue, and no, I didn't find it. It came by way of a ransom note.

BRUCE: What did the ransom note ask for?

MR. HARTMAN: It asked for pictures of Doris Day, Mamie Van Doren, Kim Novak, Vera Miles, and a picture of Marlon Brando in his Union suit.

BRUCE: Ha! Ha! Ha! Ha!

MR. HARTMAN: What's so funny?

BRUCE: Boy will they be surprised when they find out Marlon doesn't belong to the union. Although this case was a real toughie, I knew now who the guilty party was.

BRUCE: Mr. Hartman, I know now who the feen is, and with your help, I'll prove it.

MR. HARTMAN: Who stole my calendar?

BRUCE: Miss Cooper. Here is what I want you to do. You call Ms. Cooper down here on the carpet for some trumped up charge

MR. HARTMAN: I can't do that.

BRUCE: Why not?

MR. HARTMAN: I don't have a carpet.

BRUCE: Mr. Hartman, if you want to be funny, you will never see your calendar again.

MR. HARTMAN: I'm sorry, I'll do anything to get it back.

Mr. Hartman went to his closet and began putting on his coat.

BRUCE: Mr. Hartman, where are you going?

MR. HARTMAN: Out to buy a carpet.

BRUCE: If you ever want to see Marilyn again, you had better get back here and listen to my plan. You get Ms. Cooper in here in fifteen minutes. Keep her here on some pretense so I'll have a chance to search her room. It shouldn't take over ten or fifteen minutes.

1:35: I wandered the halls, giving Mr. Hartman a chance to get Ms. Cooper to his office.

1:50: I went to Ms. Cooper's room and knocked on the door. There was no answer. I opened the door and looked inside. The room was empty. I went into the room and began looking around. In her desk, I found what I was looking for, her diary.

1:55: I went back to Mr. Hartman's office. When I got there, Mr. Hartman was bawling Ms. Cooper out for not giving me an A in French. When Mr. Hartman saw me, he really started laying it on thick.

MR. HARTMAN: And how could you possibly give such a kind, considerate, upstanding, and responsible a boy as Bruce a 2 in citizenship? Come on, Ms. Cooper, anymore of this sloppy grading could cost you your job.

Ms. Cooper gave a big sigh, and tears started streaming down her cheeks. I took my hanky out of my pocket and gave it to her. Ms. Cooper looked at me through tear-filled eyes.

Ms. COOPER: I know you didn't put him up to this, Bruce. No one who is kind enough to give his hanky to a crying lady could ever be that cruel.

BRUCE: I gave you my hanky because you were splashing on my shoes.

Ms. Cooper was mad. I don't know how I could tell. I guess it was the way she threw my hanky on the floor and began jumping up and down on it. She then hurried out of the office.

MR. HARTMAN: Did you find anything?

BRUCE: Yes, I have her diary right here.

We read the diary from cover to cover, but there was no mention of Marlon Brando. Mr. Hartman began chewing me out for barking up the wrong tree. As I hung my head in shame, I noticed a letter laying on the floor. I picked the letter up. It must have fallen out of Ms. Cooper's diary. The letter explained everything. In the letter, Ms. Cooper told Marlon she was in love with him and would do anything for a picture of him.

MR. HARTMAN: Bruce, how did you now the thief was a woman when all the evidence pointed to a male crook?

BRUCE: I deducted that since the ransom note asked for four pictures of females and only one picture of a male, it was really to throw us off guard.

MR. HARTMAN: But how did you know it was
    Ms. Cooper?
BRUCE: I saw her in a movie once. The name
    of the picture was Desiree. When she saw
    Marlon, she went ape. That's how I knew
    she had a crush on him.
MR. HARTMAN: Bruce from what school did you
    get your superior detective training?
BRUCE: Elementary, my dear, Mr. Hartman,
    elementary.

The end.

My thoughts returned to the present. That seemed like so long ago. I never got the urge to write anything again until now. I don't consider the songs God has given me as my writings. Those are gifts from God. I guess as I'm writing this, this is also a gift from God. Every positive thing we do is a gift from our heavenly Father.

The last picture from the past that I can remember about Val and I happened one Saturday afternoon. We were riding around town when we saw these two girls walking. Val knew the one girl. Val turned the car around and went back to where they were walking. We asked them if they would like to go to the drive-in movie with us that night. The one that Val knew said she would go out with Val. The other one said she would have to ask her mom and dad. Her mom said if it was all right with her dad, it was all right with her. We took them down where her dad was working. He guessed it would be okay.

Our date was certainly not love at first sight. As far as I know, Val never saw the girl he dated again. I really didn't know how to take the girl I dated. I don't think she said over two words all night. Did she like me? Did she not like me? I didn't really know. The next day though, I got a chance to find out. It was Sunday, and I was out driving around by myself. I don't know why, but I happened to drive by her house. She and her family had just gotten out of church. She was just getting ready to go into her house when I drove up and asked her if she would like to go to my sister's house and see their pet fox. She said she would go in the house and check with her parents and see if it was okay. They said she could go with me. It's kind of funny. She told me later she thought I asked her if she would like to go with me and meet Pat Fox. She thought, *Boy, he's got a lot of nerve asking me to go and meet another one of his girlfriends.* When we got to my sister Joan's house, her husband, Evart, was sleeping. When he woke up, I introduced him to Sandy. As they were talking, he found out her last name was Genter. He told her he had relatives by the name of Genter. When they got done comparing names, they decided they were cousins. Even though this relationship didn't start out on the strongest start, Sandy and I have been together almost sixty years. I guess that just proves that you don't have to have love at first sight, just a relationship that has love and respect for each other, and it can last a lifetime.

As my thoughts snapped back to the present, I saw Val's sister, Arlene; she has changed over the years. I would never have recognized her if she hadn't told me who she was. We looked at some of his pictures they had on a board. Oh how many years had slipped by since Val and I spent so many days and nights together. So long, my friend. I hope over the years you came to know Jesus. It would be great being reunited serving Jesus.

My son Bruce and his wife, Sheila, were in a pinch for money. They talked it over, and Bruce decided to sell his guitar. Bruce didn't want to sell, but he felt he didn't have any other options. He put flyers out and set the price at $600. My nephew John, in Florida, said he would like to buy it. Bruce said the price was $600 with $100 down and the balance when he received the guitar. Bruce got the $100, so he packed the guitar and shipped it out. Bruce never received any more money from John. That wasn't the end to this story. John sold Bruce's guitar and bought a different one. I was steamed. You can do things to me, that's one thing, but when you hurt my family, that's another matter. The feelings I had bordered on hate. God spoke to me and said, "Bruce, you take care of the loving, and I will take care of the judging." I learned a long time ago the only way you can possibly win is to do what God tells you to do. I put John on my prayer list. Sometime later, God spoke to me again. "Bruce, did you just put John on your prayer list, or are you praying for his salvation?" God already knew the answer; he just wanted to hear it from me. I told him he was just on my prayer list. God wanted me to pray for John's salvation. I told the Lord I would pray for John's salvation.

Some days later, Sandy's sister called. "You know what happened?" she said to Sandy "Someone broke into John's apartment and stole his guitar."

When I heard that, I said, "Thank you, Lord, for your faithfulness." God was not only faithful in not letting John keep what didn't belong to him; he wanted John's uncle to be faithful in praying for John's salvation.

In the movie *Chitty Chitty Bang Bang*, they sang a song. In this song was the phrase "Out of the ashes of disaster grow the roses of success." God doesn't cause bad things to happen to us, but he will allow them to happen. Sometimes, it's for our own good.

CHAPTER 10

As I continue to write, I am going to use stories and excerpts from books from other people. I hope you don't think I'm using what other people have written to make me look good, because it's not. I started writing at first to give God honor and glory that He so richly deserves. As I continue on and end this story, nothing has changed, because it's not about me; it's about our awesome God. It always has been, and it always will be.

In the book *Angel in the Rubble*, it tells the story of Genelle Guzman-McMillan. She worked in one of the twin towers. On September 11, 2001, she was working on the sixty-fourth floor. When the first plane hit the tower she was working in, it felt like an earthquake had struck. She was one of sixteen that stuck together. They started to walk down because the elevators weren't working. They got to the thirteenth floor when the whole building came down. She was trapped under concrete and steel beams. Her whole life flashed before her. As a child, she was brought up knowing and serving God, but she had drifted away from God. She had come to the United States on a green card from Trinidad. When her card had expired, she stayed rather than going back home. She was living with a man outside of marriage. She was partying every weekend. She knew God couldn't be very proud of her. She said, "God, if you get me out of here, I'll change my life and start living for you again."

God did get her out, and she did keep her promise to the Lord. She started going to church, she got baptized, and she got married to the man she was living with, whom she also loved. She got her immigration status taken care of, and they allowed her to stay in this country. I forgot the most important thing. While she was still trapped in the rubble, she asked God's forgiveness. God allowed her to go through all that happened to her not only for her own good but also for his honor and glory.

Sometimes we go through pain and suffering to benefit others. One couple was going to have a baby. They were overjoyed. They had prayed for a baby for a long time, and now it was becoming a reality. When the baby finally came, they were on the mountaintop and could hardly contain their emotions. The baby they had prayed so long for was finally here. The doctor told them they had a healthy baby boy. The next day as she was talking on the phone to her husband, the doctor came into her room and told her that her baby was in trouble. No matter what they did, the baby's condition kept getting worse. The doctor then left her room. The mother couldn't believe what the doctor had just told her. She was heartsick. She kept praying, "Let my baby live. Let my baby live." Later that day, her baby died. She was in total disbelief. How could God allow this to happen? The next day, she was released from the hospital. It was like she was living a bad dream. She came to the conclusion that God had to have a reason for letting her baby die. She was just going to leave it in his hands.

Two months later, a lady down the street was going through a heartache of her own. Three years ago, she had to watch her husband suffer and die of cancer. Now her only son had been in an awful car crash and was killed. She had lost the will to live. So many kind-hearted people came and tried to comfort her, but they couldn't. Oh, they said they understood, but they really didn't understand. How could they? None of them had suffered the loss of a loved one.

The lady who lost her baby took some tea and cookies down to the lady. She embraced her and told her she had just lost her baby and understood the grief she was going through. They became friends, and the lady who had lost her baby was able to tell her how God sent his son to suffer and die for our sins so that someday we could live with him in heaven.

Now she understood why God let her baby die. What a great, understanding, and loving God we serve.

Matthew 5:48 says, "Be perfect, therefore, as your heavenly Father is perfect." This baffled me for a long time. I always thought that we would never be perfect until we were changed in a twinkling of an eye when we received our new bodies. I know I'm far from perfect. In 1 Corinthians 13:13, it says, "And now these three remain faith, hope, and love. But the greatest of these is love." These are the most important things we have now, but when we get to heaven, we won't need faith or hope, because there will already be in heaven the things we are hoping for and have the faith we will be there some day. The only thing that will follow us into heaven will be our love.

So isn't it love God wants us to perfect while we are here? If we back up to the five verses before Matthew 5:43–47, this is what they say,

> You have heard that it was said, "Love your neighbor and hate your enemy. But I tell you Love your enemies and pray for those who persecute you that you may be sons of your Father in heaven. He causes his sun to rise on the evil and the good, and sends rain on the righteous and the unrighteous. If you love those who love you, what reward will you get? Are not even the tax collectors doing that? And if you greet only your brothers what are you doing more than others? Do not even the pagans do that?"

Then comes verse 5:48, "Be perfect, therefore, as your heavenly Father is perfect." God must be telling us to perfect our love.

In Colossians 3:12–14, it says,

> Therefore as God's chosen people, holy and dearly loved, cloth yourselves with compassion, kindness, humility, gentleness and patience.
>
> Bear with each other and forgive whatever grievances you may have against one another. Forgive as the Lord forgave you. And over all these virtues put on love, which binds them all together in perfect unity.

In 1 Timothy 6:6–7, it says, "But Godliness with contentment is great gain. For we brought nothing into this world, and it is certain we can carry nothing out." There is one thing we get to carry out with us, and that is our love.

God may not always be pleased with the things we say or do, but we must never lose sight of the fact that God's love and salvation is meant for everyone. That doesn't mean everyone will be saved, just those who call upon Jesus to save them through the saving power of his precious blood.

During all of our married life, Sandy and I lived from paycheck to paycheck. We never put any money away for retirement. The main reason was there was never enough to save. I did get money when the company retirement plan was stopped. We put that money into a savings account. Six years before I retired, Straits Steel and Wire Company started a 401 K plan. At first, I didn't think there was enough time to bother with. The more I thought about it, I decided it was fifty-fifty plan up to 4 percent. I thought I might just as well get everything out of the company I could. The last six years, I signed up for the 401 K. After I turned sixty-five, I could work full time and draw social security too.

We started putting my social security check in the credit union account and live on our paychecks. Work started slowing down because of NAFTA. I was asked to retire. That was nice ways of saying my services were no longer required. Because I was let go because of NAFTA, I was able to draw both social security and unemployment for one year. We lived on unemployment while putting the social security checks into the credit union.

I don't want to forget Sandy who was also working. She didn't always work full time, but many times her income kept us afloat. We went from paycheck to paycheck to more than enough. It went back to when God taught us to tithe. It's all about trusting Him. Luke 6:38 says, "Give, and it will be given you; good measure, pressed down, shaken together, and running over will be poured into your lap. For with the measure you give, it will be given you." God's law works!

In January 2008, our pastor asked us if we would take over the church food pantry. I wasn't at all sure I wanted to do it. The lady and her husband, who ran it before, never had enough money. They found it necessary to ask their pastor to take up an offering for the pantry. Besides, they put their own money into it. I asked our pastor if he would take up an offering if it was necessary. He said yes he would. Reluctantly we agreed to operate a citywide food pantry within our church. The last thing the lady who ran it before said to Sandy was, "Make sure they know it's your food pantry." I'm not sure if she meant that people were trying to tell her how to run the food pantry or if it was a pride thing. No matter, we put God in charge of His food pantry from the very start. We have been in charge of His food pantry for four years. Many people have donated money to God's food pantry, and we have never had to ask for a penny. That's what happens when you put God in charge. I've had to look back and see in the beginning how I looked at people instead of looking at how great our God is. I had to ask God's forgiveness. While most food pantry shelves are empty, our shelves are full. We keep moving stuff around trying to make room for the food that is coming in. Praise our great and awesome God! You'll never know Jesus is all you need until Jesus is all you got.

CHAPTER 12

In October 2012, I had an appointment with my dermatologist, Dr. Paula Provost Blank. We had to go to Traverse City to keep that appointment. The night before, the Lord told me he wanted me to pray with Dr. Paula. That made me awful uneasy to say the least. I don't mind praying with my friends, but to pray with someone I hardly know, that's another thing. I always see her once a year, and she is always busy. That night and the next morning, I made several excuses why I couldn't pray with her, but when all was said and done, I knew I would do it. I learned a long time ago that when God tells you something, you'd better listen.

We arrived in Traverse City the next day for my appointment. The sun was shining, the birds were singing, but I was still nervous. I had paperwork to fill out, and then the nurse called me back to a room. The moment of truth had arrived. Dr. Paula came into the room, greeted us, and then checked me over. She told me everything looked fine. She filled out paperwork and began to leave the room. I asked her if she had a couple minutes for me. She said she did and asked what she could do for me. I told her God had told me to pray with her today. She said she would be glad to pray with us, and we prayed several minutes. When we finished praying, Dr. Paula had tears running down her cheeks. She said she was glad I waited until she was done looking me over or she wouldn't have been able to see me. She hugged us, and we left her office. A few days later, we got a nice letter from Dr. Paula. She thanked us for taking our time to pray with her. It really made us feel good.

Today, October 1, 2013, I had to return to see Dr. Paula for my yearly checkup. The trip from Ludington to Traverse City was awesome. The sun was shining, and the trees were showing their colors. What a beautiful day. The only thing to spoil the day was all the papers I had to fill out when I got there. With all the papers finished, Dr. Paula came into the room. She said she was so glad to see us and gave us a hug. Dr. Paula told us the prayer last year was perfectly timed. It wasn't long after we prayed with her when family friends asked them to spend the night with them at their cottage. They took their dog with them, which seemed like a mistake. The dog got sick all over the cottage floor. They felt they should take the dog home so they could care for him there. They found out later, there had been a gas leak, and they could have gotten pretty sick if they hadn't taken their dog home. God's timing is perfect, and sometimes He uses other people praying for us to help keep us safe. He also used it to get me out of my comfort zone. Nice job, God, you killed two birds with one prayer.

About four months ago, my left leg started bothering me. I went to our family doctor, and he sent me to the hospital to get X-rays. I went back to the doctor in a few days when the test results came back. The doctor told me that the results showed I had severe arthritis in both hips. He asked me if I had anything to take for the pain. I said I had Meijer arthritis medicine. He told me to take them, plus he gave me a prescription for a cream to rub on the place where it was painful. It wasn't only a short time later my shoulder started hurting, and I was sent back to the hospital to have X-ray of my shoulder. When the results came back, I was informed I also had arthritis in my shoulder. The doctor told me that because the arthritis in my hips was severe, I might have to see the surgeon someday.

I started taking the arthritis medicine two in the morning and two before I went to bed. I also rubbed lidocaine where it hurt the worst. If I had a good day, I wouldn't take any medicine. After about two weeks, I noticed I hadn't taken any pills or rubbed any lidocaine on my skin. It's been a couple of months now, and I have not been having any pain. The only conclusion I can come up with is God healed me. It will be about two months before I go back to the doctor, and I can hardly wait to tell him that I don't have to go see the surgeon. I'm going to tell the doctor that my own personal physician took care of my arthritis. I can only imagine how this old body would feel if my heavenly Father wasn't looking after me. What a wonderful God we serve.

As I've tried to let you see all the things God has brought me through and all the things God has done for me, I haven't touched much on the things He's brought my wife and sons through. God has brought my lovely wife, Sandy, through so much! She has had a hysterectomy, gall bladder removed, bowel surgery twice, ruptured disc in her back, a knee replacement, pneumonia several times, allergies to almost everything, cancer two times, and arthritis in her hands and neck. With all of this, she remains a loving wife and mother. What a blessing she is!

Bruce is our oldest son. One time he cracked his neck playing football. The doctor told Bruce to remain inactive for a while. If he would be hit just right again, he could be paralyzed for the rest of his life. Sometime later, Paul got mad at Bruce and told us Bruce had been out sliding. God protects the innocent and the foolish.

Also as a young boy, Bruce was running toward the front door. I guess he was going to open the door and go outside all in the same motion. When the door didn't open, Bruce put his arm through the glass, slicing his arm. It bled profusely. Bruce was lucky; no, God had his hand on him. Bruce did not sever an artery or a tendon.

As a young man, Bruce was pitching in a softball game. A power hitter from the other team hit a line drive. The ball hit Bruce in the chest and knocked him down. When Bruce got up, he was spitting blood. I ran out to him, and when I saw the blood, I said to him, "Come on, Bruce, I'm taking you to the hospital."

"No," he said. "I'm going to finish the game." He did finish the game, and then we took him to the hospital. The doctor told him he was a lucky boy.

"When someone gets hit like this, they usually die," the doctor told us.

Another time Bruce was coming home from Grand Rapids during a storm. He no more than arrived when we heard on TV that the Hart Bridge collapsed. Bruce must have driven over that bridge within fifteen minutes of the collapse.

Only a couple a years ago, Bruce was again driving in a storm; we phoned his home to see if he had arrived home all right. We told him about the tree that had fallen on a car and killed the driver. He said, "I know, I was the third car behind him." Some unbelievers would say that Bruce was just lucky. I say, "Our great God protected Bruce."

When Paul was about one year old, he was running a temperature of 105 degrees. Sandy took Paul to the doctor who gave her a prescription and sent her home. When I arrived from work, I showered and held him over my shoulder while sitting in the rocking chair. All of a sudden, something didn't seem right. I brought him down off my shoulder, looked into his face, and saw that his eyes were rolled back in his head, and he was convulsing. We rushed him to the hospital. I. wasn't sure we weren't going to lose our little boy. The nurses had to get his temperature down, so they laid him in ice chips. The poor little guy turned blue and cried. Paul had pneumonia. He recovered and did not have any brain damage. Praise the Lord!

When Paul was in his teens, he broke his arm while playing football. He also had an accident while playing softball. He slid into second base and hit his head on the hard ground around the base. He didn't jump up quickly but laid there. We ran out too see what was wrong and found him convulsing. I held his head in my lap and began talking to him. I didn't know if he could hear me, but I wanted him to be assured everything would be all right. What a helpless feeling for a father! All I could do was to talk to him and pray for him, not knowing what is wrong or what the outcome will be. Again, he had a full recovery.

Paul travels so far to work every day—driving about two hundred miles each day. Twice, he has had rollovers on black ice. While driving in the fog, he hit an electric pole. You could expect quite a bit of injuries from these three accidents, but Paul walked away from all of them with only minor injuries. Thank you, Jesus!

CHAPTER 13

Do I have any regrets in my life, maybe a couple.

I regret not coming to Jesus sooner.

I regret some of my behavior while I was still listening to Satan.

I regret not being a very understanding father as my boys were turning into young men, getting on their case about their long hair, their music, and their earrings.

I guess I was trying to fit them into my mold instead of helping them through this tough adjusting time in their lives. I guess they made it through the transition in spite of my failure. Bruce and Paul turned into fine men. They have given Sandy and me two wonderful daughters-in-law and five awesome grandchildren.

I asked God, way back then as a teenager, to send me someone to love so I could have a home too. He did more than that—He has given me a family anyone would be proud to call theirs.

What a great God we serve! I don't know how much time I have left or what will happen to me in that time. Only God knows what's in store for us. I can only look back and see how God has taken care of me and my family, then look forward to see how he cares for us in our remaining days.

In the book *Taken* written by Dee Henderson, I found God talked about. It surprised me because I saw the movie *Taken*, and God wasn't mentioned once unless maybe as a curse word.

In the movie, Matthew Danes's daughter and a friend went to Paris on spring break. They were kidnapped by human traffickers. Dane went to Paris and got his daughter back. In the book, his daughter was six years old when she was kidnapped and got her back when she was sixteen.

The book starts when Dane is a speaker at a convention. He felt satisfied with how his presentation—Best Practices in the Dialogue between the Police and Victim Families—had gone. As he arrives back at his hotel room, he finds a young woman sitting on the floor by the door. This woman heard how he had rescued his daughter and helped her readjust to normal life. She had been kidnapped when she was sixteen and was held for eleven years. She had gotten away because they thought she was dead and wanted him to help her.

I want to let you read a little from Danes's first conversation with Shannon.

"I didn't know the day freedom would come, Matthew, but I've been preparing for this for a few years, and I've a working to-do list. I tried to anticipate what I could. I knew once I reappeared matters were going to unfold quickly with a lot of pieces moving around. That's why I sought out your help, not because I couldn't handle this, but because I didn't want to deal with all these different events on my own. But the details themselves—most of them I've thought through."

"That's helpful to me Shannon," he would figure out how to get on the same page with her. "Very helpful." Her reply told him she thought she was ready for this. That actually gave him a good clue for where the first emotional crack would appear. She was braced and ready for what she had anticipated, but she had little margin right now for the blindside surprise. Protecting her from one, buffering her against such a thing when he couldn't prevent it—that would be a good outcome if he could pull it off. "I like that about you. The fact you planned this, are facing head-on the difficult items like finding a doctor. I don't know how best to say this...but I'd like to be your backup when you have more of those hard things on your list to do, if you'll allow me to do so." "I'd appreciate that." "Good. Now, let me ask a different question." "Sure." "You meet with your brother. Then you meet family members as you choose to do so after that. Talk to me about the broader picture. Do you want to see a particular friend from high school? A best friend? Would it be helpful for you to have a conversation with someone from your church?"

"Friends from high school will have gone on with their lives. Catching up with them can wait until the news has died down. There are some I'd like to call in the first day or two after this goes public, say hi in person. But friendships have a natural lifespan, and a best friend will have to reappear to fit my present situation."

She shifted in her seat to face him. "I'll enjoy being back at church, but which congregation I settle with depends on where I'm living, and I doubt I decide that question for some months. While I'm still unknown, I wouldn't mind going to services to sit in the balcony with you if we can avoid the church my family attends. Jeffery is a known face right now and I'm not interested in calling attention to myself. But that wasn't the substance of the second question you asked. You wanted to know if I would find it helpful to have a conversation with someone from my home church—have someone to talk with about the tough questions my experience has raised."

"Yes."

"Your daughter struggled with her faith because of what happened." He hesitated. "I'll let my daughter talk to you about that one day. I won't try to characterize her concerns. But it was a topic which did prompt a lot of conversations."

"Thank you for that—for respecting Becky's confidences. You gave an interview when your daughter was still missing. You were asked the question: "What has this done to your faith? You answered along the lines of, "God is good, and I love him. Right now, God is permitting a very hard thing. Why, I don't know, but I still trust Him. God will help me find my daughter." That interview and statement stuck with me. That's one of the reasons I tracked you down. Do you still think that way, now that Becky is home and you now her story?"

"I do. I struggled with trusting God in the first years after she was home, knowing what Becky had gone through. But I still believe God is good and I do love Him. It came back to what I knew to be true. My faith today is firm in that."

"I'm glad. To your question, no, I don't require a conversation with someone from my church, someone to help me with what this did—or did not do—to my faith."

He looked over. "Your faith survived what happened?"

"Yes. You seem surprised."

"I think I am. Puzzled at least."

"My relationship with God is fine."

"Seriously?"

"I'm a cactus, Matthew. Not an orchid. They're beautiful, but they can't handle heat or a tough environment. The circumstances throughout my life have made me who I am. I can plan. Strategize. Think across long periods of time. Put me in a room with those who hate God, and I can still thrive. God has made me into a tough, battle—hardened believer. I am very grateful to have those eleven years behind me. But I used them. I chose to survive with my faith intact. I chose to come out strong and together. I endured, and now I'm going to thrive. I don't expect life to be easy. I do expect God to be there with me. He was during the last eleven years."

Matthew hesitated. "I'm not sure what to say."

She smiled "I'm my own person, Matthew, with my own strengths and weaknesses. You just bumped into one of my strengths. leap think for myself. Hold onto decisions I've made. I believe certain things about God. I know certain things about God. A family of smugglers didn't stand a chance of changing my mind about that, no matter how. horrifying my circumstances became." Shannon briefly went quick, then added "I can tell the differences between the acts of a man and the acts of God. That's why I still believe. I could always tell the difference."

"You were hurt. Bones broken...and other violence, "he said, alluding to what he suspected had happened. She didn't flinch from the comment. Her gaze held his when he glanced over. But it was the controlled gaze he'd seen in Atlanta, the enforced calm.

"It was men who hurt me, not God."

"God allowed it," Matthew said quietly, going to the heart of his daughter's struggle with God.

"He did. And I wondered for a time if God still loved me." Shannon was silent for a long moment, then smiled. "I used to wonder how I'd answer this question once freedom came and someone asked me about God. It's not a conversation I think I want to have very often. But would you listen to my long answer, let me see if it makes sense to you?

"I'd like to listen to whatever you want to say, "Matthew replied, surprised she was willing to further open this particular door with him.

"I realized something, probably about year two, "Shannon said, "that changed how I thought about God and what was going on. I'd like a featherbed world where falling out of a tree didn't break a bone. Where a guy couldn't land a blow on someone smaller than himself, where no one ever got to touch me without my consent. That's the world I would have created. But God decided to create a world where free will was more important than no one ever getting hurt. There must be something stunningly beautiful and remarkable about free will that only God can truly grasp, because God hates, literally abhors, evil, yet He created a world where evil could happen if people chose it. God sees something in free will and choice that's worth tolerating the horrifying blackness that would appear if evil was chosen rather than good. I find that utterly remarkable."

Matthew nodded slowly as he considered her answer. "From the very beginning, all the way back to the Garden of Eden, human beings have had a choice" he agreed, beginning to sense how she'd settled this matter for herself.

"Can you imagine how marvelous Eden must have been? God walking with Adam and Eve in the evening where they could talk face-to-face. God gave Adam and Eve that free will and a choice. He gave them one warning: eat of any tree that is here, including the wonderful tree of life, but don't eat from the tree of knowledge of good and evil." Shannon paused. "I wish Adam and Eve had thought more about what knowledge meant. Eve saw it as a good thing, to know more. But how do you really know something? You experience it."

Matthew looked at her, realized how pale she had become, and reached over to cover her hand with his. He felt her suddenly shiver. "I got a nasty taste of what evil is like these last few years, "Shannon went on. "The sad thing about evil...we did this to ourselves. It wasn't God's plan. God expected, fully intended, for Adam and Eve to obey what He had said, to leave the tree of good and evil alone."

Shannon turned her hand under his, gripped it, seemed to seek and find comfort from that contact. "Were Adam and Eve's children, reaping their decision. We chose the knowledge—the experience of good and evil—and we found out just how bitter and dark evil really is. We experience it now. That's our reality. There's probably not a person alive who wouldn't want to go back and see that decision changed, now that we have tasted how bad it turned out to be. My faith survived because I realized God didn't want this for us, He never had. I'm passionately looking forward to a new Heaven and Earth where only good exists once more." Matthew drove for three miles after Shannon finished her answer before he said, I'm stunned at your reply."

"Why?"

He quoted a couple of her statements back to her, about Adam and Eve choosing knowledge, which brought about the experience of good and evil. "That's pretty deep theology, Shannon."

"Time was heavy on my hands; I had some time to think."

"It's wisdom." Matthew hesitated. "But it's also abstract. God didn't stop men from hurting me. Does that fact make God not good? I concluded that God was suffering as I was, but He didn't want to end free will or bring the world to judgement yet, He permitted what happened. People hurt me, not God. He didn't divinely rescue me from the world I live in, even though that was within His power. He simply walked each hour and day of it with me, and promised me that justice was coming. And as hard as it was to accept, I reached the point I could accept it. God is Immanuel—"God is with us" It's enough truth to rest on. God had been acting honorably throughout history regarding what He wants. We're the ones at fault. God is good. And I still really, truly like Him. My relationship with God is fine."

Matthew drove further in silence, thinking about what she'd said. At last he offered, "Thank you Shannon."

"For what?"

"For convincing me better than anyone ever has that there is such a thing as a tough God-fearing, bring-it-on woman left in the world."

She burst out laughing.

He smiled. "I hope my daughter turns out a bit like you one day."

"God help you if she does, "Shannon replied with good humor.

The conversation felt mostly finished, and Matthew accepted that. "I'm glad it's okay with you and God."

"So am I. I'm not saying there weren't some very dark stretches between myself and God.

We certainly had our moments. But we worked through them as time passed—that had to happen early on, Matthew, or I wouldn't have survived. The strength to survive, the planning, the long-term game theory, the strategies—that was God and I getting inside the dynamics of this group. I did it with God. So you can mark off your list wondering about my relationship with Him."

"You're going to love my list then, because the next item on my agenda is to take another nap."

He chuckled. "At least you don't snore."

She looked distinctly embarrassed. "I hadn't even thought of that."

"You look…" he began, then stopped! and shook his head. Adorable, cute, lovely—all of them fit what he could say about how she looked when she slept, yet they weren't appropriate to the conversation. "I'm glad you feel like you can rest when we travel. Chicago is going to take a lot out of you quickly. I'd rather you arrive as refreshed as possible." He offered a reassuring smile. "Get some more sleep while you can, Shannon. It's the best use of your time right now."

She shifted around the pillow and settled back in the seat. "Thanks for listening to my long answer."

"I'm blessed by it," he said quietly; She'd understood God at a deep level. She was right. Her relationship with God was fine.

That makes you think, doesn't it? I'm glad I serve a God who never changes. In spite of free will, he is always there for us. Lord, help me to appreciate you more.

The book of Revelations tells us this old, sin-filled world will pass away, and a new heaven and a new earth will come down to take its place.

A new world where sin and death will be no more.

A New Jerusalem will come down, and Jesus will be king for evermore.

We will go to live with Him for evermore.

He promised to wipe away our tears.

What a wonderful thought—no more sadness once we go home.

This is a Reader's Forum written by Eric Jefferies titled "An Open Letter to an Alien." I would title it "An Open Letter to God."

> Welcome to planet Earth, you've arrived in time for Earth Day. Most visitors are surprised at how fast they're still moving after landing here. If you could ride a bullet fired from a high powered rifle, you'd be going about 2,000 MPH. But don't try that unless you are unsatisfied with your current velocity of 67,108 MPH; that's our orbital speed so that we don't get sucked up into our sun.
>
> We've been able to map some of the universe; but we humans really have no idea where we are, where we are going, or where it ends. The Earth is forecasted to continue as it has for recorded history; so you might as well join us

natives as we sit back, enjoy the ride and do our best until we die.

You give us hope, because after looking light years in every direction this is the only planet known to have life. But we don't just have single cell organisms with cellular machines that would have boggled Darwin's mind; we also have 170 ton blue whales with a heart as big as a cow and everything in between. Our D.N.A. stores a million pages' worth of data in a single molecule— an efficiency unrivaled by computers. We're still discovering animals that are miles under the ocean where the pressure would make a nuclear submarine look like a crushed pop can.

I know it sounds arrogant, but I Want to draw your attention to the highest life form— me and about 7 million of my friends. We're not always the strongest, the fastest or the wisest but we're the smartest.

Humans are also the only life form capable of believing in things we can't see or prove, like gods and aliens. This capacity for faith has created many different cultures on our planet.

No matter where you go on Earth, mosquitoes, dogs, and elephants interact the same; but not humans, some of us are in "left field," "right field," or "out of this world." One thing we have in common is that we all think we're right and have a desire to be loved.

Now that you're here, you'll want to consider which culture you'd like to live in. We have nations that believe that there is no god, nations that believe their leader is god, nations that will kill you for speaking against their god, and nations that let you believe anything as long as you pay reoccurring fees called taxes.

I know I'm biased, but I'd like you to stay here in Mason County, Michigan. You'll like the beautiful lakeshore and we could use some help. Like many cultures, ours has been changing; I recently talked with some veteran peace officers who notes some disturbing trends over their decades of services.

Our population has shrunk but our jail population has grown. More people are using prescription to get higher instead of healthier. Domestic violence has increased; that's where family member hurt instead of love each other. Criminal sexual conduct has increased; that's doing things that most animals won't do. Most jailed for C.S.C. can tell you how pornography fed their perversion.

Murder has increased; that's killing people for interfering with your life. Our court has even dealt with people killing a baby and a police officer. It doesn't help that some video games virtually condition us to mow down people like grass.

More people have also been murdering themselves and don't seem to care that they'll be missed by someone who loves them, even if that person hadn't been showing it very well. Perhaps you know a way to make the prosecutor's case load a part-time job. It's not like the "Sky has fallen" on everyone, but it's starting to fall on those with destructive habits and we could use some help thwarting the next potential tragedy or broken heart in our community.

Coincidentally, most crimes are committed by people from broken families. It's not the child's fault when a parent does wrong, but they grow up with the effects and could use some extra help. There's got to be a better way for parents to spend divorce fees which can rival the cost of a child's education. If even half that money was spent on flowers, date-nights, baby-sitters and counselling, I'm sure most of these marriages would be savable. After all, if people liked each other enough to make a marriage covenant and babies, there's got to be hope most of the time.

There's a new movie that's supposed to let us know "Heaven is for Real"; but it would just be nice if more people lived like they were planning to go there.

I know it's been a couple thousand years since you've been here; but Easter season seemed like an appropriate time to ask for some extra help this year. You couldn't get enough votes to be elected president, but maybe when people get to know you better, they'll respect you enough to only use your name when they're talking to you or about you. That way they wouldn't say "Oh My God" any sooner than they would say "Oh My Buddha" or "oh my mother."

Please give us more of what makes life worth living—love; it's the only thing that makes tough times bearable or keeps our free will from becoming a free—for—all.

Thanks for the offer of forgiveness that Easter brings and for giving us a planet worth celebrating on Earth Day. Amen

There are people out there, who spend their whole life constantly searching the heavens to find new star systems, new comets, and new planets. They recently found a planet just like earth except for one thing. It was too close to its sun and was too hot to sustain life. Wouldn't their time be better spent searching for the one who created the heavens? In their wisdom they become as fools.

Someone once said "Life is like a wild goose chase—without the goose." It can feel like a search for something that's always elusive. In the midst of the search, however, a book as trustworthy as the Bible assures us that the Creator of the universe cared so much for us that he came seeking after each of us.

In a world of loneliness, despair, and rejection, the Bible offers hope and encouragement. In the words given to a blind beggar named Bartimaeus: "Cheer up!...He's calling you." Yes, the Creator cares for you! With that awesome truth in mind consider the words of astronaut Guy Gardner, who said this about what he had learned when he saw the marvels of the created universe in outer space: "It's very hard to think this must have happened by chance...You realize at the same time that there had to be a Master Designer, a Creator of this planet, and to me that makes life all the more special. Because that tells me that instead of me being something that just came along in the course of time to live and die, that instead of a meaningless existence, I have someone—who cares for me—who made me and cares about me. Someone I can go to with my troubles, and my cares, and my joys.

Now imagine God's creativity. Of all the things we don't know about the creation, there is one thing we do know. He did it with a smile. He must have had a blast. Painting the stripes on the zebra, hanging the stars in the sky, putting the gold in the sunset. What creativity! Stretching the neck of the giraffe. Planting the giggles in the hyena. What a time he had. Like a whistling carpenter in his workshop, he loved every bit of it. He poured himself into his work. So intent was his creativity that he took a day off at the end of the week to rest. And then as a finale to a brilliant performance he created man. With his typical creative flair, he began with a useless mound of dirt and ended up with an invaluable species called human. A human who had the unique honor to bear the stamp "In his image."

At this point in the story, one would be tempted to jump and clap. Bravo, encore, unmatchable, and beautiful, but the applause would be premature. The Devine Artist has yet to unveil his greatest creation.

As the story unfolds, a devil of a snake feeds man a line and an apple and gullible Adam swallowed both.

This one act of rebellion sets in motion a dramatic and erratic courtship between God and man. Though the characters and scenes change, the scenario repeats itself endlessly. God still the compassionate Creator, woos his creation. Man the creation alternately reaches out in repentance and rebellion.

It's within this simple script that God's creativity flourishes. If you thought he was imaginative with the sea and the stars, just wait until you hear what he does to get his creation to listen to him. For example:

- A ninety-year-old woman gets pregnant
- A woman turns to salt a flood blankets the earth
- A bush burns but doesn't burn up
- The Red Sea splits in two
- The walls of Jericho falls
- The sky rains fire
- A donkey speaks

Talk about special effects: But these acts, be they ever ingenious still can't compare with what was to come.

Nearing the climax of the story, God motivated by love and directed by divinity surprised everyone. He became a man. In an untouchable mystery, he disguised himself as a carpenter and lived in a dusty Judean village. Determined to prove his love for his creation, he walked incognito through his own world. His callused hands touched wounds, and his compassionate words touched hearts. He became one of us.

Have you ever seen such determination? Have you ever witnessed such desire to communicate? If one thing didn't work, he'd try another. If one approached foiled, he'd use a new one. His mind never stopped. In the past, God spoke at many times and in various ways, writes the author of Hebrews, but in these last days he has spoken to us by his Son.

But as beautiful as this act of incarnation was, it was not the zenith. Like a master painter, God reserves his masterpiece until the end. All the earlier acts of love had been leading up to this one act.

The angels hushed and the heavens paused to witness the finale. God unveils the canvas and the ultimate act of creative compassion is revealed.

God on the cross.

The creator being sacrificed for the creation. God convincing man once and for all that forgiveness still follows failure.

I wonder if while on the cross the Creator allows his thoughts to wander back to the beginning. One wonders if he allows the myriad of faces and acts to parade in his memory. Did he reminisce about the creation of the sea and sky? Did he relive the conversation with Abraham and Moses? Did he remember the plagues and the promises, the wilderness and the wonderings? We don't know.

We do know, however, what he said, "It is finished."

The mission was finished. All that master painter needed to do was done and was done in splendor. His creation could now come home.

In the beginning God created the heavens and the earth. That's what it says in the Bible. "God created the heavens and the earth." It doesn't say God made, or God built, or God produced, or God developed. No it says God created the heavens and the earth. That one word says a lot. Creating is a lot different than constructing. The difference is pretty obvious. Constructing something only engages the hands while creating something engages the heart and soul. You've probably notice this in your own life. Think about something you've created, a painting, a song, a few lines of poetry you never showed anyone, or even the dog house in the back yard. How did you feel about that creation? Good, proud, ever protective? You should. Part of you lives in that project. When you create something, you are putting yourself into it. It's far greater than an ordinary assignment or task. It's an expression of you.

What if it is the truth? Creator really does care for us and is seeking us, then everything now depends on our willingness to trust Him. If Jesus is God in the flesh, then apart from Him we will never know real joy, real meaning, or real peace in life. He is our Creator and He seeks a personal relationship with us. Have you responded to His sacrificial love with faith and accepted His invitation to everlasting life, forgiveness, and peace?

Carefully consider what the Bible says:

For God so loved the world that he gave His only begotten Son, that whoever believes in Him should not perish but have everlasting life. For God did not send His Son into the world to condemn the world, but that the world through Him might be saved. He who believes in Him is not condemned; but he who does not believe is condemned already because he has not believed in the name of the only begotten Son of God (John 3:16–18).

May the Love of our heavenly Father, and the salvation through his Son Jesus, and the guidance of his Holy Spirit be with you now and forever more!

15
CHAPTER

This is the end of my story at least that is what I thought. How can you not say there's more to this story when God does something so special for you that you want the whole world to know? The only trouble is I already have an ending for the story.

What perplexes me is this, do I start a new story? Do I go on from the finish of this one even though the ending I think is great? It was getting late, so I decided to go to bed and think it over in the morning.

I no more than hit the pillow when God gave me the answer. He said, "Bruce, you can put it wherever you please, my glory never ends." So I guess I will continue on from where I stopped. The only trouble I can foresee is finding a new ending. I guess I will let God give me another ending.

So I will keep on writing knowing there will always be more to write as our great God keeps covering us with his awesome love. So here goes with another chapter in my life showing His love for me even though I'm so imperfect.

16
CHAPTER

It all started one night. I woke up with a sharp pain in my meaty part of my back. As I got up, the pain was even worse. When I began moving around, the pain was gone. The next few nights, it was more of the same. I told Sandy what was happening. Sandy told me that I should make an appointment and see the doctor. True to form, I told Sandy, "In a few days, it will get better."

Well, it didn't get any better. In fact, it got worse. After about three weeks, I called and set up an appointment with the doctor. Guys, listen to your wife. Next to God, they will give you the best advice.

Monday, February 14, I arrived at Dr. Susan's office for my appointment. The nurse checked my vitals and told me Dr. Susan would be right in. True to the nurse's words, Dr. Susan came in in just a few minutes. She had another lady with her, and she said the person with her was a doctor in training and asked if it was okay if she sat in on the visit? I told her it was all right. She began asking me questions where was the pain, how long I had the pain, was it a dull pain or a sharp pain. And how bad was the pain. I told her the pain was in the right side of the meaty part of my back, and I'd had it for about three weeks. I also told her it was a sharp pain and on a scale of 1 to 5 it was a 6. She had me lay on the table and started checking me out. When she got done poking and prodding, she raised my right leg straight up in the air. There was a slight twinge, but it wasn't bad. She then proceeded to lift my left leg up, and I didn't even have a twinge at all. She then told me I could get up, and that's when the fun started. When I started trying to get up, the pain was so strong I struggled, and Dr. Susan and the other doctor had to help me sit up. Dr. Susan said she was going to send me for an ultrasound and a CT scan. She also gave me a prescription for a painkiller (Norco).

Tuesday, February 21, I went to the hospital for my ultrasound. It was about 8:00 a.m. when I checked in with the lady getting people registered in for what they need done. When she got all the questions answered, she gave me a folder with my paperwork in it and told me where to go. Sandy and I sat down and waited for the nurse to come out and call my name. They came out and called several names, but my name wasn't one of them. Sandy looked at my folder and pointed to the time. It was 8:00 all right, but it was *p.m.* not *a.m.* I couldn't believe it. It wasn't the time. I couldn't believe it was the fact I didn't see it was *p.m.* The registration lady hadn't noticed it either.

At 8:00 p.m., I came back to the hospital once again. It wasn't long before the young lady doing the ultrasound came out and got me. She had me lay on the table. She then proceeded to tell me what she was going to do. First, she was going to check the kidney and then the bladder. She went ahead and checked the kidney. It took a lot longer than I thought it would. She repositioned me and then did the bladder. When she was all done, she told me I could get up. I tried to get up, but it was a real struggle. The pain was so great it took me several minutes to get up. The young lady that had done the ultrasound looked like she didn't know what to do. When I finally sat up, she asked me if I was okay. I told her I was, and she led me out to where Sandy and I was sitting. It had been a long day, and Sandy and I were so glad to leave the hospital and go home.

Friday, February 24, we went to the hospital again. This time, it was to have a CT scan done. It was scheduled for 9:00 a.m., and this time, I made sure it was 9:00 a.m. and not 9:00 p.m. that was written on the paper. When my paper had been checked, Sandy and I went and sat down waiting for them to come and get me for the CT scan. This time, it was a man who came to take me for the procedure. He told me what he was going to do and gave me something to drink. I don't know what it was for, but it gave me a warm feeling. I had to lie on a table again. This table moved, and when it moved, it put me in a position so they could take pictures. It took a while, and when they were done, the fellow told me I could get up. I tried to get up, but it was too painful, so the one who had taken the pictures helped me up.

February 27, Dr. Susan called and told me the results of the test came back and showed I had a kidney stone. She told me she couldn't do anything for me. It was not in the range of her practice. She told me she was making an appointment for me with Dr. Reum, the urologist.

March 6, 10:30 in the morning, I arrived at Dr. Reum's office for my appointment. After the nurse took my vitals and left, Dr. Reum came in. He was quick to tell me that the pain that I had wasn't caused by the kidney stone that they saw but was the same one that was there back in 2012. He said that it was only about a one-eighth of an inch, and it hadn't grown much if any. He said he felt the pain was being caused by either arthritis or maybe by the cyst that I have on my kidney. He drained it in 2012 when it was the size of a softball, but maybe it has filled up again. "You wait here, and I will go look at the results from the CT scan and see if it has filled again.

When he returned, he told me it had filled to the size it was when they drained it. Dr. Reum told me he was going to make an appointment with the kidney doctor for me.

March the 9, noon, I went to my kidney doctor's office. It was a short wait, but then my doctor came out and invited me into his office. He asked how I was doing and did the usual small talk. He then told me that my pain was not being caused by the cyst. If it was being caused by the cyst, it would be constant and not just while I was lying down or trying to get up. He said it had to be caused by arthritis. He said he would send the other doctors a message saying the pain was caused by arthritis, and they should have an MRI done. He said that until they got this thing figured out, I was still to keep taking Norco for my pain. This visit was on a Thursday.

All the visits to three doctors had not done anything for my pain except Dr. Susan Persson had given me a prescription for Norco for the pain.

The following Wednesday, I had not heard from even one of the three doctors. Wednesday night, Sandy and I went to prayer meeting. I told them who were present about my pain and how I saw three different doctors and each one had a different idea of what was causing my pain. I also mentioned that it was almost a week since I had heard from even one of them.

One of the ladies in attendance asked if I had gone to the altar and had people lay hands on me and pray for me. I said I hadn't, but I would like us to do that. We went to the altar, and the people laid their hands on me and prayed for me.

Since I only took Norco just before I went to bed, I hadn't needed to take any during the day because I didn't do much lying or getting up during the day. For the next two days, I noticed I didn't even get a twinge, so I decided to see if I could get along without Norco, so I stopped the Norco. From then until now (which is several months), I have not had any trouble with my back. I think you will agree with me; I don't know what was wrong with my back, but God healed it. Isn't God awesome?

April 3 at 9:30 was my next visit to see Dr. Susan. She asked me how I was, and I told her I was great. She asked me how my back was, and I told her how I had seen all three doctors and each one had a different idea as to what was causing my pain. I told her how after I saw the kidney doctor, a week went by, and I hadn't heard from any one of the three. Dr. Susan rolled her eyes as if to say we botched that one. I went on and told her how God had healed my back. She said she was glad for me. Our meeting was a short follow-up, and then we prayed, and Sandy and I left.

During my prayer time, I not only worship God and tell him all my pray requests, but I try to listen to him and what He tells me. I need to back up for a moment. Since God healed me, I have been telling people I come in contact with how God healed me. Perfect strangers I sit next to in the hospital or people I meet in the grocery store or even people I meet on the street, I tell how God has wonderfully healed me.

God has shown me how it hasn't happen but was a building process. First He got me out of my comfort zone by having me pray with Dr. Paula. Like I said before that praying with Dr. Paula was like killing two birds with one prayer. My boldness continued to grow by my praying with Dr. Susan. Granted she had a need for prayer, but so do I. By meeting other people's prayer needs, it helps my boldness in telling others how God has healed me. Isn't it wonderful how God works within us sometimes when we're too blind to see how He's helping us grow?

Not only does He help us to grow, but He will heal us if we allow Him to. Matthew 21:22 says, "All things whatsoever you shall ask in prayer believing, ye shall receive." The word this whole prayer hinges on is *believing*. If you don't believe God is going to heal you, He won't. Proverbs 3:5 says, "Believe on the Lord with all your heart and lean not on your own understanding." Jesus was touched by the woman with an issue of blood. She had been to doctors for twelve years. They took all her money, and yet she was not healed. She felt in her heart if she could but touch the hem of Jesus's garment, she would be healed. She touched His garment and was instantly healed. Jesus told her, "Because of your faith you have been healed."

While Jesus was still speaking, someone came from the house of Jairus the synogues' ruler. "Your daughter is dead," he said. "Don't bother the teacher anymore."

Hearing this, Jesus said to Jairus, "Don't be afraid, just believe and she will live."

When he arrived at the house of Jairus, he did not let anyone go in the house with him except Peter, John, James, and the child's mother and father. The reason for this was all the others believed she was dead. Jesus took the child by the hand and said, "My child, get up!" Her spirit returned, and at once, she stood up. Jesus had healed her because those in the room had faith.

The other morning, I woke up and the part of my back where I had had the sharp pain in my back was hurting. It wasn't as sharp or as strong, but it was still there. After about half the day was gone, God spoke to me and said, "What you're feeling is just the devil trying to make you believe I hadn't healed you. I told the Devil to leave. He wasn't welcome here." I haven't had that pain since.

I also remember some time ago that I had a pain in my leg. I went to the doctor, and Dr. Brian sent me for a CT scan. Dr. Brian got the results and told me I had severe arthritis in both hips. When I told Dr. Susan, she said, "You might have to see the surgeon." It wasn't long after that that I had a pain in my shoulder. The doctor also said that was arthritis. God must have healed these also because I'm not having any pain from them. It's funny how God can meet your needs, and you sometimes don't realize it until much later if at all.

Here I am with pen in hand again. It's one o'clock in the morning and I'm wide awake. I guess it's no wonder why I'm still awake. I took a nap after supper. I guess being in the twilight of my life, my body has its own timetable for when it needs to rest.

It also makes me wonder where all the years have gone.

That young man Bruce, our first son, has reached the fifty-year mark. He and his wife, Sheila, have two boys and one girl and one grandson.

Wow, that makes Sandy and me great-grandparents. I don't know about Bruce, but it makes me feel extremely old.

Then there is our youngest son, Paul. He has two girls and one grandson. Even though he's four years younger than Bruce, he's starting to get gray streaks in his hair.

I find that no matter how old you get, you still don't think of yourself as old. When I look in the mirror in the morning and see that old guy, I say, "If that old guy is going to live here, he ought to be paying some of the bills."

Earlier, I talked about my sister June. In the year of 1993, June entered Tender Care. It was a place for adults to be cared for. I think June liked it there even if she wouldn't admit it. She loved the nurses and the care she received. She also got along well with the other people there. June wrote poems and loved to recite them for whoever would listen. She also continued to make her beautiful rugs.

One day when Sandy and I went up to see June, she was sleeping. I called to June and shook her a little bit, but she wouldn't wake up. I put my hand in June's hand, and she clamped down on my hand so hard it began turning purple. I did finally get my hand free after quite a struggle. June never did wake up.

Three days later, we received a call from Tender Care that June had died. I wonder if June knew that she was dying when she held my hand so tight. Maybe she did and didn't want to be alone. Only God knows.

Years before, Sandy became June's guardian. She had foresight to start a funeral fund at a bank. When June died, there was enough money in the fund to give June a very nice funeral, but June was not there. She had already gone home to be with Jesus and the home she had been cheated out of for so many years before. June will no longer be confined to a wheelchair. She will be walking with Jesus, maybe telling him one of the poems she wrote or telling him a funny story she heard. June would always say when we were getting ready to leave her, "It's not good-bye, it's just so long until we meet again." So, June, it's just so long until we meet again.

CHAPTER 18

In Mark 10, Jesus says, "Let the little children come onto me for such is the kingdom of heaven." I believe that Jesus wants us to be children to him in prayer. I have several children on my prayer list. One was a fifteen-year-old. He had cancer and was terminal. After he had died, I met his grandfather and was talking with him. He said, "A short time before he died, he told me, 'Grandpa, I've never felt so close to God in all my life.'"

A three-year-old girl and an eleven-year-old both had cancer. They both had a piggy bank in a credit union. Every time I went into the credit union, I would put one dollar in each of their banks. That may not seem like much, but I'm sure it helps. I went into the credit union one day, and the three-year-old girl's bank was gone. My first thought was that she had lost her battle with cancer. I asked one of the tellers why the little girl's bank was gone. She told me the little girl was now cancer-free, and she didn't need the help anymore. I was tickled pink. The eleven-year-old boy just doesn't seem to get much better. He had to go to Texas for more treatments. The organization that had his piggy bank there got the bank emptied so they would maybe have some money for gas. I'm sure they were as surprised as I was when they counted almost $1,000. I believe wholeheartedly that Jesus increased those dollar bills, just like he fed over five thousand people with one little boy's lunch. Praise You, Jesus.

I have a brother and sister combo on my prayer list. I would say they are about twelve and fourteen years old. They live with their grandparents. They seem like good kids. I've heard that they had a terrible childhood, and I think that's probably true because the girl tried to kill herself. The family has moved to Florida, so I don't see them anymore but still keep them in my prayers. They need God's protection.

I have one little girl in my prayer list. I don't know her or her parents, but I know her grandparents. The grandfather said when she was asked what she wanted to be when she grew up, she said she wanted to be boss. Her grandfather said that the truth of the matter is that at five years old, she already is the boss. Her parents never say no to her.

I pray for one little boy and his family. He's five years old, and that little boy has gone through so much. He has so many problems; in fact, he doesn't have much of an intestine left. His mother has just been saved, and I'm hoping his father will also. For that little boy, although he has physical problems, the best gift God could give him is Christian parents.

I have two boys and one girl on my prayer list. They are brothers and sister. I pray that God will continue to bless this Christian family. The father has to drive a long way to work. I pray that he will find a good job closer to home. If he had a job closer to home, he could spend more time with his family. The kids are good kids, and I'm sure they would love to have more time with their dad.

19
CHAPTER

Y ou may remember me talking about my granddaughter Megan. She is grown now and has a son, Quinten. He's so cute. He's seven months old and such a happy baby.

When Megan was a young girl, the family got a dog. He was a golden retriever. He was such a good dog, but like humans, dogs have their little quirks. One was he didn't like to be put on a chain outside, and the only other one I know about was he was afraid of big trucks. By the way, his name was Milo.

Milo loved to ride in cars. When the family wanted us to dog sit, they would just say, "Milo, you want to go to Grandma and Grandpa's?" He would race you to the door.

One time that Milo was at our house, I tried to take him outside and put him on his chain, but Milo planted his feet, and he would not budge. So I said to Milo, "Okay, Milo, you can stay in the house." It couldn't have been more than a few minutes and along came Sandy bringing Milo back outside. I told Sandy that I had just put Milo back in the house because he wouldn't let me put him on his chain. Sandy didn't have time to answer me when Milo spotted people walking toward us up the street. Milo bounded toward them to greet them with Sandy bouncing behind on the ground. It was a scene that would have taken first prize on *America's Funniest Home Videos* although Sandy didn't think at that time that it was very funny.

The next episode of Milo at Grandma and Grandpa's house happened one wintery day. Milo had been such a good dog as he always was. I told Milo that he had been very good, so if he wanted me to, I would take him for a walk! Well, it didn't take him long to head for his chain. It wasn't too cold outside, but the sidewalk was on the slippery side. We started walking, and we were almost to the end of the block when a big truck went by. Milo, having a fear of big trucks, turned and made a mad dash for home. I had one of two choices. Choice one, I could plant my feet and try to bring Milo to a screeching halt, which if I did that, I would wind up lying on my back. The second choice was to turn and try to keep up with him. I decided the second choice was the best one, and I took off trying to keep up with Milo. As I was running, I was also calling for him to stop, but he never did until he reached our front door. When we reached the front door, Milo seemed to be okay now, but I was huffing and puffing. That must have been another scene for *America's Funniest Home Videos*.

I was cleaning out a dresser drawer a couple weeks ago, and I came upon a paper. When I opened it up, it was a paper Megan, my granddaughter, had written in one of her classes; at the top of the page was written: "Milo Free Verse Poems 1-29-08 Reading and Writing Megan Wright." At the bottom of the page was a picture of the sun and side and front views of Milo.

In between was as follows:

> I have this golden creature. He is very close to me. We always go for walks on a warm spring morning, and in the summer we goof around with the water hose, which splashes our warm faces. In the winter, we cuddle up and we are always as snug as a bug in a rug. In the fall, we chase the dancing leaves, which dance until they lightly hit the ground. This golden creature follows me everywhere, his tail just blowing and wagging from side to side. He looks like a glob of golden hair, and can you guess what his name is? He's Milo, my dog.

At the bottom of the sheet, she drew a front and side view of a dog. I bet it was a picture of her best friend, Milo.

Two winters ago, Milo died. The family was heartbroken. I got a pick, and Paul and I started digging into the frozen ground. We had to make a hole to put Milo into. Paul and I did a lot of picking, and finally, we had a big enough hole to lay Milo in. We laid Milo in the hole and covered him with a blanket and then dirt. My granddaughters Megan and Sierra, my son Paul, and Sandy and I gathered around the grave site. There were a lot of tears, and we prayed that God had a place for a good dog like Milo in heaven. I know that God loves all his creations, so it wouldn't surprise me if he does. So long, Milo, we'll miss you. How do I know we'll miss you? Because we miss you already.

20
CHAPTER

A whole lot of time has passed since I made the remark, "When I look in the mirror in the morning and see that old guy looking back at me, I thought that if he lived in our house, he ought to be paying some of the bills, but he never does." I still see him in the morning in the mirror. I have just passed my eightieth birthday, and he seems to be looking older, but God is still blessing both of us every day.

Early one Sunday, a couple of months ago, we got a call from my nephew David who is a pastor in a church near Houston. He is a son of my half-brother David and his wife, Ruby. His dad had died quite a few years ago with a tumor on the brain. David told us his mother had just passed away. She lived a good, long life. I think just a few months ago, she turned ninety-two years old. She was a good lady and loved the Lord. I'm sure Jesus was waiting for her to welcome her home.

21
CHAPTER

This country that was once one nation under God has become a sinful nation. We have kicked God out of this nation, and his nation will soon feel God's wrath. Even those who make our laws what they are (the Supreme Court) have replaced all our laws to fit Satan's needs.

First, they took prayer out of school. Our congress can open with prayer, but I guess our children might learn to talk with God, and the children would get smarter than the adults. Jesus said, "Let the little children come onto me for such is the kingdom of heaven."

Then the court took down the Ten Commandments. If the children saw them, they might believe that they might please God by following them. Again, that would make them smarter than the adults.

The next thing the courts did was pass *Rowe vs. Wade* and legalized abortion. Once more, were those judges so dumb that they thought God would bless them for killing his kids? On the contrary, God won't bless them; He will hold them responsible for killing his children. God didn't forgive his own nation, Israel, for killing their children so are we so dumb again to think God will forgive us.

Then the court legalized gay marriages. I don't know how they can call it gay; there is nothing gay about it. God made Adam and Eve, not Adam and Steve. Homosexuality is just another attempt by Satan to counterfeit what God has made. Satan always does a poor, sloppy attempt at anything he does. What would you expect? Satan is not God; he is just another created being.

God holds the Supreme Court responsible, but he also holds this country also responsible. You may not want to believe this, but

God also holds those that are called by his name also responsible. In 2 Chronicles 7:14, it says, "If my people who are called by my name, will humble themselves and pray, and seek my face, and turn from their wicked ways, I will hear from heaven and I will forgive their sins and will heal their land." I think God is telling us we need a great revival if we want to take our country back again. We need to put God back in first place in our hearts.

I started this story with the great hymn of the church "To God Be the Glory." God told me to end it with a song God gave me, "I Love You, Lord."

> I love you Lord I love you, Lord. You've given life and love and all the world to me.
>
> I love you Lord, I love you, Lord, your mercy extends as far as eye can see.
>
> I love you Lord, I love you, Lord, I am so happy because I belong to you.
>
> I love you Lord, I love you, Lord, you make my life so new each and every day.
>
> I love you, Lord, I love you, Lord! I'll show your love to others all along life's way.
>
> I love you, Lord, I love you, Lord, you are so wonderful so marvelous to me. I love you, Lord.
>
> I love you, Lord, I'll serve you with my heart through all eternity.
>
> I love you, Lord, I love you, Lord.

> PS: There will never be a true end to this story 'til the Lord Jesus comes and takes me home.

This story started with "To God Be the Glory" and ends with a song "I Love You, Lord." As we walk through this life God has given us, may we give God all the honor and glory He richly deserves.

ABOUT THE AUTHOR

I wrote this story not to get any kind of publicity. I wrote it to give God honor and glory. In 1 Corinthians 8:1–3, it says, "Knowledge puffs up, but love builds up. The man who thinks he knows something does not yet know as he ought to know but the man who loves God is known by God.